T0208709

IN THE SPIRIT OF
SONSHIP

ALFRED PRESCOTT

WESTBOW
PRESS®
A DIVISION OF THOMAS NELSON
& ZONDERVAN

Scripture taken from the King James Version of the Bible

This book is a work of non-fiction. Unless otherwise noted, the author and the publisher make no explicit guarantees as to the accuracy of the information contained in this book and in some cases, names of people and places have been altered to protect their privacy.

WestBow Press books may be ordered through booksellers or by contacting:

WestBow Press
A Division of Thomas Nelson & Zondervan
1663 Liberty Drive
Bloomington, IN 47403
www.westbowpress.com
1 (866) 928-1240

ISBN: 978-1-9736-5372-1 (sc)
ISBN: 978-1-9736-5371-4 (hc)
ISBN: 978-1-9736-5373-8 (e)

Library of Congress Control Number: 2019901796

Print information available on the last page.

WestBow Press rev. date: 2/27/2019

Contents

Dedication vii

Acknowledgements.. ix

Introduction xi

CHAPTER ONE
The Fig-Leaf Mentality 1

CHAPTER TWO
In the Spirit of Sonship 12

CHAPTER THREE
The Emergence of the SON 22

CHAPTER FOUR
In the Image of the Son 35

CHAPTER FIVE
The Kingdom is Ours.. 40

CHAPTER SIX
The Spirit of the SON.. 49

CHAPTER SEVEN
The Spirit of Emancipation... 60

CHAPTER EIGHT
The Gathering of the Brethren 66

CHAPTER NINE
Praying in the Spirit of Sonship 73

CHAPTER TEN
Worshipping in the Spirit of Sonship 83

CHAPTER ELEVEN
The Perfection of the SON...The Season of the Manifestation............. 92

Reference List.. 101

About the Author... 103

Dedication

This book is dedicated to all seekers of spiritual truth whose inquiring minds have been imprisoned by the debilitating effects of traditional religions. Through these pages, may your understanding be released to a level of intimacy and spirit of sonship that will satisfy your inward hunger.

I also dedicate these pages to the Pastor of the "Sons of God Fellowship", Mr. Kenneth Adams and to his wife, Mrs. Gail Adams, who have labored for many years to release the truth of sonship to the body of Christ. May this book do justice to your vast knowledge, as imparted by the Holy Spirit, and to the faith and belief you have demonstrated over the years.

To all the members of the Fellowship, may these pages bring clarity and a deeper understanding of our lives in the Spirit which result in the fullness of your intimacy with our FATHER.

To the youths of the Fellowship, may you be inspired to take the task to a greater, global level of activity and usher in the greatest explosion of spirituality the world would have ever witnessed.

Acknowledgements

I give honor to the Holy Spirit for using me to write this book. Thank You for the inspiration and the grace of patience to wait on Your divine wisdom and understanding.

To my pastor Kenneth Adams I thank you sincerely for your input and advice. I also take this opportunity to thank you for your permission to use your *In Him factor* I hope my contribution within this book did justice to this vast topic.

To Najuma Banfield, whose assistance was immeasurable, I thank you sincerely. Without your help in finding the appropriate scriptures, this book would not have been the success that it is. I am forever in your debt for coming to my rescue with your laptop after my PC decided enough is enough.

To the following brethren who read the manuscript and offered advice, the level of my gratitude cannot be adequately expressed in any written format: Mr. Joel Adams, Mrs. Michellee Adams, Mrs. Tricia Jaggernauth and Mr. Ronald Constant.

I owe a great debt to Mr. Paul J. Peters to whom I am eternally grateful. Mr. Peters offered his expertise in editing the entire manuscript and because of him, the book has achieved a level of professionalism that makes it an even greater literary work.`

To all those who offered words of encouragement and support, I thank you. It is my strongest desire that this book may achieve global edification which will vindicate your belief in the wisdom released throughout these pages.

Introduction

Before everything in the physical existed there is Spirit. An entire universe made up of planets, stars, asteroids, and nebulae was conceived and birthed out of the divine purpose of a spiritual Creator. In the superiority and excellence of Spirit, Almighty God was preexistent before all things that presently stimulate our physical senses and infinitely existed in a time that cannot be measured by conventional means. For the all-powerful I AM has no beginning.

Everything, other than Almighty God, whether spiritual or physical, has a beginning (Genesis 1:1). This Supreme Being has no starting point or date of birth, for the Creator is infinite and does not need a place or specific point to occupy or control His existence or being.

This puts Almighty God in a unique position of being self-sustaining. Everything else that exists depends on and needs some other entity to sustain its existence and as a counterpoint so that it could be identified as a distinct element. Only God alone does not depend on these inter-relationships to maintain HIS personality, character, and uniqueness. But because this God is FATHER, HE has exercised HIS gracious nature in bringing other creatures into being, in the spirit and in the physical, in order that these other elements could share, be an integral part of the whole, and enjoy existence through and by the Spirit of life.

It was always the eternal will of the Father of all creation to bring into being a SON. This SON, being a fully integrated creature, is comprised of the First begotten Son of God, Jesus the Christ (Hebrews 1:6), as the Head, and mankind, the sons of God on the Earth, forming the body.

Through this supernatural intimacy, mankind was preordained to have an eternal connection with Divinity and via this spiritual arrangement, was assigned to rule and take care of the Earth, as a spiritual ambassador of Heaven.

Based on the will of a purposeful Creator, all of humanity's history and development has been a Godly orchestration to bring mankind to a condition of perfection.

Man's destiny is forever set in the heavenly decree, at the beginning:

> "And God said, Let us make man in our image, after our likeness: and let them have dominion over the fish of the sea, and over the fowl of the air, and over the cattle, and over all the earth, and over every creeping thing that creepeth upon the earth."
>
> Genesis 1:26

It was always in the destiny and purpose of creation to have an intimate amalgamation, between God, the Creator and man, conceived and developed through the direct involvement of Almighty God, in the terrestrial affairs of humanity. Mankind's eternity is linked to his true existence as a son of God.

The sonship of man is the pinnacle of mankind's existence but human beings have preferred to settle for a mediocre, pseudo-spiritual existence to hide behind their distaste for total submission to the Spirit. A part time approach to spirituality is preferable to most people. Any concept that would accommodate an occasional token prayer or an infrequent church visit but does not intrude too much into the general lifestyle of the practitioner would be readily embraced by most human beings.

These man-made institutions are perfect for hiding as they give the deceptive appearance of some formation of spiritual activity, however inadequate that may be, but does not foster total commitment to the ways of the Spirit.

But as the internal, immaterial presence cry out for a more meaningful connection, mankind must know that these hiding places cannot provide adequate cover from the Creator, as the trees failed in Adam and Eve's case [Genesis 3:8]. The eyes of the Lord can penetrate every man-made structure, every pseudo-spiritual activity, every shield man could erect, for HIS spiritual eyesight can dissect every layer of mankind's defenses even down to the spirit/soul.

A very poor decision followed by devastating actions in the Garden in Eden had initiated the development of Almighty God's eternal plan for mankind to unfold.

Even though these actions by the first couple had led to the curtailment of the Holy Spirit from preeminent and indwelling participation in mankind's life, which adversely affected his role, purpose, and identity as a son of God, through a Godly orchestration, all things would lead to the fulfillment of humanity's perfect future.

God is developing one family of spirit-beings in order to establish the supremacy of the Spirit realm in the physical realm and to eternally influence the development of all living things, under a spirit of sonship.

It has always been about the SON. The Creator had so ordained that everything must revolve around the SON. Everything was created for the SON.

Mankind, in spite of his imperfect beginning, in the Garden in Eden, was always preordained to be an integral part of this eternal sanctification and glorification process.

From the outset of the Divine declaration "Let us make man in our image, after our likeness..."(Genesis 1:26), Almighty God has always been in control of all things so that in the end of times, the Perfect SON would emerge to exercise HIS God-given authority over the earth.

ONE

The Fig-Leaf Mentality

There is a yearning within every human being which questions his presence in the universe. As he searches to find answers that would satisfy this innate feeling of inadequacy, mankind sinks deep into his day-to-day activity probing for some outlet that would fill that internal void.

All of his actions and pursuits are dedicated to answer that question that wrenches at his heart and baffles the mind: Is there more?

For all of his accomplishments, this inward hunger rages on and continues, in most cases, to be unfulfilled and unanswered. Elements of frustration, hopelessness, and loss are generated within the mind as these achievements have done nothing to quench that thirst which has attained levels of insatiability.

There are some who have achieved great feats in the history of mankind and have received accolades which have surpassed the heavens but still the yearning frustratingly gnaws away at the heart strings of the soul.

Some have believed that money would answer all things and have spent all of their lives passionately pursuing the almighty dollar, but we read about suicides and mayhem in the lives of millionaires so many times that we know it cannot be about money. The dollar evidently is not almighty.

Some people believe amassing vast amounts of knowledge is the key, but unhappiness and dissatisfaction are not exclusive to those who possess MBA's, PhDs, or the carnal thoughts of humankind's philosophies and doctrines.

Fame as well has not spurned any confidence in offering channels of unsurpassed joy and peace. So many people of renown have not led enviable lives.

It has been argued by many philosophers, over the years, that what people are really looking for is power. With all of their pursuits, individuals have been searching for something to give them power above circumstances over which, presently, they has no control: sickness, the uncertainty of the future and the big one – death, are all conditions which they endeavor to have the authority to conquer. The problem lies in the avenues human beings have decided to traverse in order to attain this power which has resulted in a complete disconnection from the Source of that capacity.

It was King Solomon in his wisdom who came to the conclusion that the pursuit of satisfaction did not reside in the attainment of material possessions, power, fame or knowledge:

> "Vanity of vanities, said the Preacher, vanity of vanities; all is vanity. What profit hath a man of all his labors which he taketh under the sun?"
>
> Ecclesiastes 1:2-3

As a king of Israel, Solomon had experienced it all: wealth, wisdom, and the adoration of many women which had given him renown to the ends of the earth. But with all this, the desire for something more was never diminished which indicated to this king of reputed wisdom that all of his accomplishments were nothing more than vain endeavors (Ecclesiastes 12:2-8).

In the maturity of the latter part of his life, Solomon had finally understood that our internal problems were a profound manifestation of an inappropriate connection to the Creator:

> "Let us hear the conclusion of the matter: Fear God, and keep his commandments: for this is the whole duty of man."
>
> Ecclesiastes 12:13

When Adam became *detached* from God, his carnal nature took precedence over the influence of the Spirit and thus Adam died, spiritually. The *breath of life* was now isolated and from then on Adam became a dying soul, physically. The true essence of man's existence is this Spirit/soul intimacy. In this respect, it is easy to see the determining factor that causes this insatiable yearning, from within, to arise.

As the soul is in constant disconnection from its true, original and heaven-bound Source and has become dependent on a physical/carnal nature for its direction and purpose, it is that spiritual presence within that cries out, as a signal for man, to seek deliverance from this ungodly arrangement.

It is this individualism and disconnection of the *breath of life* (Genesis 2:7), which has been bequeathed to every descendant of Adam, that gives most of us this feeling of dissatisfaction and lack of purpose.

Controlled by an earthly system of evil, the crux of mankind's existence is left with no choice but to exist in this naturally toxic environment. The soul has been in a constant condition of spiritual deprivation. The internal cry for ABBA and the search to reconnect gives us that empty feeling inside. Money, worldly power, fame and worldly education have all failed to deliver.

Ever since the banishment of Adam and Eve from the Garden of Eden, man has been on a quest to institute some form of divine relationship with his Creator. The problem is the influence of the carnal mind which has taken mankind in a myriad number of directions and has used various false institutions to make that celestial linkage possible.

> "And the eyes of both of them were opened, and they knew that they were naked; and they sewed *fig leaves* together, and made themselves aprons."
>
> Genesis 3:7 (emphasis added)

It was never necessary for the bodies of Adam and Eve to be protected from the elements; man at that time was not in conflict with his environment. There was no shame in being naked, as the purity of their souls gave them innocence and there was no reason to hide, due to guilt, from Divinity; but the fruit of their disobedient action resulted in self-awareness, independence from God and now facing their Creator was a strange and abnormal occurrence.

They became aware of both their physical nakedness and the loss of innocence of the soul and somehow they felt that by sewing fig leaves together it would relieve them of the guilt and condemnation exposed from within.

The capacity to maintain spiritual dominion, with the knowledge of evil, was beyond human beings, at that time (Genesis 3:22-24).

Since then, mankind has been on a quest to find the perfect 'fig leaf' which could provide a cover of comfort to mask the wretchedness of the soul and at the same time appease his inner yearning to worship his God.

This fig leaf mentality has done everything except taken man on a path leading to intimacy with God. It could never reestablish the sonship ideal in which mankind was created but still he persists with his earthly devices. Completely void of any input from Heaven, these devices that man has invented and given the name religion have been a tragedy to the spiritual condition of humanity and have taken him on a journey further away from the intimacy of the Father.

Religion is a reaction, initiated by man, which attempts to address and moderate the inward hunger.

To reach God who, in his *unregenerate* mind, had receded to unreachable heights, to capture the Holy Spirit who the carnal man thinks he can coax into intimacy, he invents idols made of wood and stone to give him something on which to focus. He knows God is somewhere up there out of his reach, severed from his senses and beyond his perceptions.

Therefore he creates belief systems with a multiplicity of rituals in the hope that God would be impressed and respond to his devotion to these self-imposed rites and ceremonies. God cannot be seen or heard from so mankind needs to authenticate his existence with a heavenly endorsement of this carnal/spiritual lifestyle.

Religion, therefore, is a formalized concoction, by the carnal ego, in order to maintain its ascendancy in the existence of mankind.

In the spirit of self-control, the ego rebels against the presence of the Spirit, and in this regard, has contrived every means necessary to retain its sway over the destiny of man.

The attitude and mindset for the carnal nature to have a say in which man should live, inclusive of his relationship with his Creator, have been in evidence from the beginning of time. It was the presiding factor in Cain's actions (Genesis 4:5-9). The construction of the tower in the city of Babel was conceived in the motive of self-aggrandizement (Genesis 11: 3-4). It led to the demise of Ananias and Sapphira (Acts 5:1-10) and it was responsible for the iniquitous behavior of Simon, the sorcerer (Acts 8: 18-23).

This rebellious spirit of self-glorification has learned to evolve, over the centuries, by formalizing itself into what is now called religion. Every religion, in contemporary times, is therefore related by having a common genesis and in an effort to create an air of legitimacy, by the construction of laws, regulations, and tenets.

As a counter to any instruction flowing down from the heavenly, man proceeds to sew *fig leaves* together, throughout the history of civilization and in a multiplicity of forms and fashions:

Mythology and Mysticism

Devoid of any divine guidance, man had regressed into creating a host of gods, semi-gods and the fabled exploits of half-god/half-man creations.

There are stories of spirits taking the form of trees and animals and before long everything in the universe was worshipped as sacred, worthy of honor and reverence: the creation taking precedence over the Creator (Romans 1:23-25).

Several ancient civilizations worshipped the sun. The evidence of this type of worship has been found in ancient African and Indian civilizations, and was the integral aspect of all the Aztecs of ancient Mexico beliefs. There are even modern-day concepts that teach the Son of God of the Bible was in reality the sun-god Amon Re, the first king of ancient Egypt.

The Orientals, particularly the Buddhists, went in a different direction by advocating that God is really a universal, immaterial realization that encompasses everything in existence. The personalized, transcendental Supreme Being of the West actually, by their beliefs, is a distortion of the universal consciousness and that all life-forms are incarnations that are evolving to escape suffering (duhkha).

Christianity

Jesus, the Christ, the promised Messiah of the Old Testament never appeared amongst the sons of men to create any religious movement. Jesus never trained HIS followers to develop any religiously doctrinal movement, in His name. His first public announcement to herald HIS divine ministry was:

> "From that time Jesus began to preach, and say, Repent: for the kingdom of heaven is at hand."
>
> Matthew 4:17

At no time did Jesus initiate any religion called Christianity. He came to introduce a spiritual kingdom that was totally opposite, in nature, to anything that existed on earth.

When the residents of Antioch first used the term Christians (Acts 11:26) they did not mean it as a term of endearment. It was meant to mock the believers and to be derogatory to their beliefs and lifestyle. So what had started in the spirit of contention was allowed to continue for the next two thousand years by the believers who had decided to adopt the name. If the idea is to be a follower of Christ as they say the word Christian means then by wisdom and truth the name the believers should have adopted is son of God as this is what Jesus is. Then by this token you truly become a follower of Christ.

At no time did the first apostles and believers call themselves Christians. They understood their position and entitlement, as sons, came from their faith in the Son of God, Jesus the Christ:

> "And because ye are *sons*, God hath sent forth the Spirit of his *son* into your hearts, crying, Abba, Father. Wherefore thou art no more a servant, but a *son*; and if a *son*, then an heir of God through Christ."
>
> Galatians 4:6-7 (emphasis added)

John, Paul, Peter and all the believers of the first century knew exactly who they were: sons of God. This was not a mere title of identification but it was the very essence of their lives which brought them into intimacy with the Father, as Jesus taught and the Holy Spirit reiterated in their minds and hearts. This is who they were and allowed every aspect of their beings to be dictated by this fact of sonship.

In all their epistles they reverberated this entitlement and rights as heirs to all the new gentile believers and converted Jews:

> "But as many as received him, to them gave he power to become the sons of God, even to them that believe on his name."

John 1:12

> "And will be a Father unto you, and ye shall be my sons and daughters, saith the Lord Almighty."

2 Corinthians 6:18

> "That ye may be blameless and harmless, the sons of God, without rebuke, in the midst of a crooked and perverse nation, among whom ye shine as lights in the world;"

Philippians 2:15

The fact that the term *son* is mentioned 534 times and the term *sons*, 53 times in the New Testament whilst the term Christian appears three times adds to the bewilderment as to why believers have called themselves Christians, over the last two thousand years.

For those who believe that it makes no difference whether we call ourselves Christian or son of God and that the two terms mean the same thing, should consider the following points:

i.   A son of God is the truest representation of how God relates to us (2 Corinthians 6:18). There is no scripture that suggests God calls us or see us as Christians. If how we look upon ourselves is in alignment with how God sees us then the power and authority of the true Church would be clearly manifested in contemporary times. Adopting a title that is outside of the will of God lessens your position, efficacy and purpose in representing God on the earth. (If you see yourself as a slave, in your mind, then you would act as a slave, with no entitled power, even if you live in a free society).

ii. The term Christian is a generic term which includes a myriad number of religious beliefs with many differences in teachings and dogma. The grouping encompasses Roman Catholics, Seventh Day Adventists, Anabaptists, and many others. So diverse is this grouping that no unity is possible as they vary vastly on many interpreted points of theology which fosters quarrels and contentions.

iii. Christianity carries and implies religious connotations with all the negativity that comes with that position: superficiality, haughtiness, self-centeredness, and falsehoods.

iv. A son of God gives us the intimacy the Father had initiated with Adam. The term itself renews your mind into the boldness necessary to live and act in accordance with divine authority.

v. A son of God means you belong to the Father as you carry His name. It should be obvious that Almighty God would not allow His name and character to come into disrepute so that the Father/son of God relationship is one based on sincerity and gentility. The sonship relationship is one that cannot be faked as you can with Christianity. Our heavenly Father would not allow it for too much is at stake.

vi. Sonship has full implications with respect to having the same nature and personality as God, the Father. Can we say the same thing for a Christian?

Christianity as a theological system has its beginnings in Rome and not in Jerusalem. It was created as a compromise to appease many factions of people who made up the population of the city at that time, thus placing it within the domain of the *fig leaves*. Several traditions and rites peculiar to the region were incorporated into the teachings of the Apostle, Paul, so that many different beliefs would be preserved and many people would be satisfied that their ideologies would not be lost to history.

An example of this toxic intrusion into the gospel of the kingdom of God as expounded by Paul and the early believers is the spring festival of Easter. This festival was practiced as worship by the Anglo-Saxons peoples to and named after their goddess, Eostre.

Their beliefs and accompanying customs were blended into the beliefs of the followers of Christ who commemorated the resurrection of Christ and the Jewish Passover on 14 – 15 Nisan. To accommodate the Anglo-Saxons, the date of the festivities was changed in the 2nd century to the Sunday following 14 – 15 Nisan. This simple date change had far-reaching implications as it encouraged many other changes to be brought in, over the years and thereby altering the original intent and spirit of the belief.

This new religion which now mirrored the roman way of life had major differences with what was taught in Jerusalem and Palestine. Even though the name of Jesus Christ remained at the core of the believers, the concept of the kingdom of God was changed into Roman Catholicism and papal supremacy. The sonship of man was replaced by adherence to religious do's and don'ts. The freedom to worship in the spirit and truth of Christ was obliterated by artificially created boundaries; organizational regulations, rules, ordinances, and laws; and bondage to denominational thinking.

Christianity as a religious practice could never embrace total spiritual intimacy as accommodated by the Fatherhood/sonship relationship. Created under a compromising spirit, the true power that positions the believer constantly within the bosom of the Father is beyond the scope of Christianity.

From its inception, Christendom has always promised more than it can possibly deliver. Its deceptive nature has beguiled many church attendees, over the years, leaving a long line of frustration, despondency, and apostasy in its wake. A great number of adherents of the Christian faith have been left with feelings of un-fulfillment after the many years of devotion to the never-ending rituals and denominational traditions which have failed to satisfy the inward spiritual hunger.

The problem is escalated as new converts in Christ, who are baptized as sons of God, into the kingdom of God are now indoctrinated into the theology of Christianity, thereafter.

Christianity cannot usher you into the kingdom of God. The kingdom is of a spiritual nature while Christianity is of a carnal nature, having its origin on the earth.

Protestant Religions

In 1517 Martin Luther had initiated a movement that questioned the validity of the Roman church and the infallibility of the pope. With several excesses in papal authority the break away from roman control and the creation of reformed religions were inevitable. But the reformation was only superficial since the inherent falsehoods of religion were never addressed. Initially, the idea to oppose the roman ways of worship was cemented in the quest for righteousness but the *fig leaf* mentality went into overdrive and the super religion of Rome was replaced by several religions that stumble on to this day.

The modern day believer sees himself as a Pentecostal, as a Seventh day Adventist or as a Roman Catholic or after so many of the denominations in operation, today. This is in direct contrast to the Church of Jesus Christ as the adherence to the various religious tenets encourages disunity and division and is further exacerbated by the antagonistic attitude of the practitioners as they continually struggle to prove the supremacy and exclusivity of their individual faiths. The Church of Jesus Christ was founded on sonship (Matthew 16:16-18) and advances the cause of oneness as there are no divergent beliefs and spirits, within sonship, to cause a schism within the movement; as in heaven, so on earth.

Every civilization throughout the history of mankind has invented its own form of religion, full of rituals, laws, customs, moral, and ethical codes, myths and legends.

These various religious practices with their many rites and ceremonies espouse the justification of the believer by works. The religionist with no access to the mind of the Creator has to resort to trying to impress God by indulging and devoting himself to the endless rituals. The believers are led to think that if they do not faithfully commit to the practices of these devotional acts, no response from Heaven is possible.

But a son of God knows that the only way he can impress his Father is by faith and not by dead works (Ephesians 2:8-9). He allows the righteousness of God to gain continuous access to his heart and mind and totally surrenders all to the Creator, and in this regard, he assumes the heart and mind of Christ, as his innate mind is totally annihilated.

Despite the sincerity of the believer, religion by its very nature cannot bring the adherents into the closeness necessary for true worship. Religion originated and belongs to the earth and has never had any input from the heavenly realms.

The power that humanity is searching for cannot be found in religion. That inward hunger that continues to plague and haunt mankind cannot be satisfied by the various *fig leaves* being practiced and adhered to in today's world. Being a son of God, on the other hand, places you right where you need to be – in the bosom of the Father. The power we seek comes from within as the presence of the Spirit supersedes the temporal nature of fleshly sicknesses; the hope that is generated in Christ makes the future something to be embraced with joyous anticipation; with the resurrection of our Lord and Savior, Jesus Christ, death is forever conquered by the sons of God (John3:16).

The soul of man was created to be in complete fellowship with the breath of God and as its source of direction, fulfillment, purpose and destiny, the essence of man must be in constant intimacy with the Spirit of the Giver of life – Almighty God. Humankind has been out of touch for far too long. The soul has been in a state of spiritual starvation for too long. Nature continues to be held captive owing to the long anticipated manifestation of the sons of God (Romans 8:19). Man must return to his rightful sonship position and discard all aspects of the *fig leaf* mentality.

TWO

In the Spirit of Sonship

There is no doubt that everything God had done, since the downfall of Adam, was directed towards the coming of Jesus, the Christ to the earth. As the only begotten Son of God, HE is the zenith of all creation and is the ultimate reason why all created things exist and by His Spirit all things have their make-up:

> "For by him were all things created, that are in heaven, and that are in the earth, visible and invisible, whether they be thrones, or dominions, or principalities, or powers: all things were created by him, and for him; And he is before all things, and by him all things consist."
>
> Colossians 1:16-17

In this regard, any plan God would have set in HIS infinite mind must have included the active participation of the Son, for it is HIS creation to restore. Besides, there is no time that Father, Son, and Holy Ghost never worked together, in complete unison.

In order to prepare the world for HIS Son's appearance, and the future emergence of the SON, Almighty God had kept a spirit of righteousness actively engaged in worldly events; Noah, Abraham, and the nation of Israel have all foreshadowed the advent of the Lord of all creation and have all made their indelible contributions to the progressive advancement of the Creator's mission and vision for all existence.

We have already been alerted towards the responsibility of divine representation which was given to man. In spite of mankind's continued disobedience, Almighty God would not divert from this all-inclusive arrangement; The Creator would always include mankind in HIS plan to permeate the earthly domain with HIS kingdom sovereignty. Man remains the object of Almighty God's attention.

Before Jesus walked among men, no bona fide son of God occupied the region of the earth, after Adam. But in order to keep the sonship ideal actively engaged in the minds of men, The Ancient of Days had used certain individuals by immersing them in a spirit of sonship.

By way of a definition, in the spirit of sonship, there is no perception of separation, in spirit, between God and His sons, in the mind of the son.

This is very difficult for humankind to grasp as we are continually reminded of how unholy we are.

We have an enemy whose duty it is to flash indiscrete actions from our past, in our minds, and keep us focused on the shame of our former lives and not on the potential greatness of a hopeful future.

But a son of God knows that as the Holy Spirit lives in him, his past has been erased by the grace of his Father and he does not have to condemn himself for what has already been committed to the sea of forgetfulness.

In the newness of a transformed life, the son of God knows that he is so intimate with his heavenly Father in a way that allows him to share the same thoughts and actions of Divinity. The Father shows the son the contents of His mind and the son follows in agreement (Luke 10:22).

In most cases, this is a synchronization that does not require any praying and fasting to hear or to know the will of Father. The son of God automatically knows and acts in accordance.

A religious mindset cannot easily process this as we have been groomed to believe that man could never be so closely knitted with God. The Creator is too holy and it is only through a long-distance grace, we are allowed some level of divine guidance.

But in the spirit of sonship the son is imbued with the nature and character of the Father and allows these heavenly attributes to dictate his presence on earth, as evidenced by Christ-like thinking, motive, attitude and movement.

In addition, a son of God recognizes that his internal nature has been transformed into the same spiritual make-up as his heavenly Father. He can now relate to the Creator as ABBA. Almighty God is now his true Source. He no longer has any allegiance to this carnal world.

MOSES

One such person who had been singled out for this celestial experience was Moses.

In the spirit of sonship, Moses developed a level of boldness in his many face-to-face encounters with Almighty God. Moses never showed any intimidation, fear, or apprehension and had always stood upright as one whose inalienable right it is to be in the presence of the incomparable God of Abraham, Isaac and Jacob. One such encounter clearly illuminates this fact:

> "And the Lord said unto Moses, I have seen this people, and, behold, it is a stiff-necked people; Now let me alone, that my wrath may wax hot against them, and that I may consume them; and I will make of thee a great nation. And Moses besought the Lord his God, and said, lord, why doth thy wrath wax hot against thy people which thou hast brought forth out of the land of Egypt with great power, and with a mighty hand? Wherefore should the Egyptians speak, and say, For mischief did he bring them out, to slay them in the mountains, and to consume them from the face of the earth? Turn from thy fierce wrath and repent of this evil against thy people."
>
> Exodus 32: 9-12

The Deliverer of the Israelites was about to destroy all of the Jewish people who had forsaken Him by fashioning a man-made object to worship in HIS place. But Moses speaking as one who was blessed with unlimited confidence managed to *change God's mind*. When one considers that this was the Creator of all things, to whom Moses was relating, it is remarkable the kind of boldness the son of man exhibited in this episode,

Even though it is well known that it is impossible for God to change

His mind, for HE foreknows all things, it is extraordinary the level of intimacy a son of God experiences with his heavenly Father.

Showered by a spirit of sonship, Moses showed no fear in dealing with a Father-figure and not the Terrible God his fellow Jews came to know I AM as.

With sincerity of heart, the man of God, Moses' motive was not enveloped in arrogance but in upholding the reputation of the True and Living God towards the surrounding nations (Exodus 32:12), and in preserving the promise God had made to HIS people so that the Jews could trust Him for future times (Exodus 32:13).

This is the crux of the spirit of the son whose boldness is generated by a pure heart. From this perspective, there is no attempt to conceal your inner self from Almighty God, as Adam had done. The sonship truth makes you free from all guilt and self-condemnation.

The Creator always checks the motive of our actions. HE loves a pure, grateful and righteous heart (Psalm 51:6, 17) and always responds in the positive in the reflection of His own heart:

> "And the Lord repented of the evil which he thought to do unto his people."
>
> Exodus 32:14

KING DAVID

Another servant who was singled out to contribute to the divine movement of God was David.

David had a God-like heart (1 Samuel 13:14) which made him into the perfect candidate to receive the spirit of a son. Living by the dictates of this spirit, David never settled for the ordinary, accepted ways of doing things for God.

Blessed with an innovative mentality, David always looked for new ways to improve the worship offered to his God. In the spirit of creativity, the king of Israel danced before the Lord with a righteous freedom that transcended all traditions and norms.

As one who never allowed his growth and spiritual enhancement to be truncated by the opinions of others, David's uninhibited bodily movements caused a stir among his fellow Jews (2 Samuel 6:14-16). The reaction by his wife, Michal is typical of those who pay more attention to carnal issues in the place of freeing themselves in the spirit.

In the spirit of sonship, immersing yourself totally in the presence of God always supersedes the workings of the material mind. Quizzical stares from onlookers or the eyes of contempt from others never factor in with regard to your personal and closely-knitted relationship with Divinity. Who you are through your worship, praise, and prayer become a lifestyle experience leaving no room for the opinions of others.

In this episode, David had no regard for the myopia his contemporaries were struggling with as the extreme joy of escorting the Ark of the Covenant superseded the self-centeredness of the city's residents.

In the spirit of sonship creativity, David altered the direction and scope of praise and worship of his day. By adding instruments to accompany the voices of the worshippers, David was able to reform the religiously comatose flavor of the praise into an ecstatic encounter of celestial heights. This gave the participants a freedom of expression that truly puts them in contact with the bliss of the heavenly realms (1 Chronicles 15:16).

In likeness of your heavenly Father, the spirit of a son of God blesses you with an innovative and creative mind that challenges the orthodoxy and stretches the imagination to unforeseen levels. You do not settle for how things are done just because that's the accepted way for ages, but with a celestial height of vision, you follow the supernatural innovations of the Spirit.

The son of God is certainly not against tradition and definitely does not go after change for changing sake. However, the pioneering mind of the son does not accept norms solely based on habitual or traditional usage. He moves in tune with the Spirit who discards old redundant ways which do not fit in with the demands of a new season or move of Divinity.

When the Creator declared "Let there be light", it was in the Spirit of originality that changed the order of things that had existed in an immeasurable time and birthed novelty into a new reality.

In likewise fashion, the sons of God envisage things not as they appear to be but with a futuristic eye, they naturally look for ways and means to improve and evolve the normally accepted ways of convention.

Always faced with the objections of those who are stuck in a religious quagmire, those whose lives are driven by the sonship spirit, push on proving and confirming the endorsement of their motives by the Spirit.

> "The Lord forbid that I should stretch forth mine hand against
> the Lord's anointed; but, I pray thee take thou now the spear
> that is at his bolster, and the cruse of water, and let us go."
>
> 1 Samuel 26; 11

With King's Saul relentless pursuit, together with his three thousand man army, to kill God's appointed king and his band of six hundred men, the demise of David seemed certain.

It seemed to be a sure thing that the king of Israel would not have relented in his campaign of hate, until the threat of his reign and royal legacy was eliminated by David's death.

But David immersed in the spirit of sonship, as he was, conceded from the temptation to take the reigning king's life, even when that perfect opportunity presented itself, (1 Samuel 26:7-12).

This is even more amazing as David had, on a previous occasion, spared the king's life (1 Samuel 24:1-11). Even then the king persisted with his maddening desire to shed innocent blood.

It is impossible for the heart of a son of God to harbor any bitterness, hate or resentment, for any prolonged period of time, even against those who swear to your downfall.

In the spirit of sonship, the heart of the son of God recognizes the underlying hurt of others and does not react to the resultant public display of animosity, as people lash out against the alienation they feel inside.

Thus, the spirit of the son could only direct the heart to extend compassion to those who are dedicated to your downfall (Matthew 5: 43-48).

There are so many believers who are secretly elated at the demise of a brother or sister. Given the opportunity, in the dark, they would thrust the knife deeper within the backs of those who have fallen on bad times, at the same time exhibiting concern, in public, for those brethren.

In the spirit of sonship, a genuine desire is generated to see all, progress and prosper, brethren and enemy alike.

JOHN the BAPTIST

In order to usher in the fullness of the kingdom of God and subsequently the reign of sonship to the earth, John, the Baptist, had to come full of the Holy Ghost (Luke 1:15). As an exceptional individual, John's convictions posed a serious threat to the stability and acceptance of the religious atmosphere and hierarchy in his time. As the precursor of the eminent, Messiah, John challenged his contemporaries to discard their old ways of worship, to realign their method of thinking, and thus prepare their hearts so that they could be in a position of freedom to accept the Savior of Israel and qualify for entry into the kingdom of God which was close at hand.

With the exception of Jesus, no other man exemplified the characteristics and personality that emanates from the sonship spirit, as John the Baptist did.

> "And as they departed, Jesus began to say unto the multitudes concerning John, What went ye out *into the wilderness* to see? *A reed shaken with the wind*? But what went ye out for to see? *A man clothed in soft raiment*? Behold, they that wear soft clothing are *in kings' houses.*"
>
> Matthew 11:7-8 (Emphasis added)

In the wilderness

Nothing about John the Baptist was traditional. He was totally unorthodox and was completely different to the times in which he was activated. In the spirit of Messianic reforms and teachings which John was about to introduce to Israel, he had to be separate and divorced from the old rabbinic traditions. If this was not so then he would have settled for a life in the Pharisee sect and resigned to reciting the laws of the Torah in the various synagogues of Palestine.

But the Spirit demanded a departure from the traditional as this new period of transformation was about to sweep across the spiritual landscape of Israel. The priesthood in operation, at that particular time, could not gratify the high requirements of supernatural advancement necessitated by this new season. In that regard, the Spirit drove John into the wilderness as a means of separation from the mediocrity of what was being dispensed as spiritual upliftment and from the established hierarchy of the day.

John who was in unison with the change in season never allowed the illusory honor of the old ruling sects to hamper the revivalist spirit of the time and at several occasions took the opportunity to expose these pseudo-spiritual blockages of progress:

> "But when he saw many of the Pharisees and Sadducees come to his baptism, he said unto them, O generation of vipers, who hath warned you to flee from the wrath to come?"
>
> Matthew 3:7

Even John's apparel and diet represented a departure from the norm which he employed to assert his independence from the establishment (Matthew 3:4).

So many believers disqualify themselves in establishing their calling through the spirit of sonship. They do not wish to *rock the boat*. They want to be friends with everyone shying away from controversial matters and trying to fit in with everyone else's agenda, but as the Spirit motivates you to represent the truth, you run the risk of clashing with a few well instituted egos.

Those who have been in the limelight for a long time and have had it easy for so long and who no longer speak the truth of the Gospel will oppose you, as you make a stand for the purity of God's word.

As you depart from the triviality of the time, speaking the undiluted word of the truth, you may find yourself outside of the popular trends of the day (a voice crying in the wilderness: Matthew 3:3).

You must have a love for God more than the accolades of men. Like John, you must flow in the spirit of sonship, placing the work of God above everything else, even at the expense of your popularity among men.

A reed shaken in the wind?

Not because something is popular and trendy means it represents the truth of God. In John's time, it would have been suicidal to come up against the traditional, pharisaical approach to the Mosaic Law. This was the accepted way which people believed epitomized the will of Almighty God. It was ingrained in every Jew that the priesthood in John's time, was the only way that exemplified the righteousness of God and so anyone who opposed this way was in fact opposing Moses and all the Patriarchs.

For someone who resisted this tradition of thousands of years would have either been a lunatic or a man of strength who does not depend on the views of the majority to inform his convictions. Even as a minority, John certainly was no *reed shaken with the wind*. He was a man of substance not bending or yielding to any prevalent trends. The Spirit set him on a path and no banishment from society could have made him divert from his righteously-driven destiny.

The spirit of sonship gives you a strong personality to resist the urge to succumb to the crowd even if it means being ostracized or ridiculed by the accepted leaders of the religious fraternity.

You possess the mental fortitude to stand on your own in the face of continuing pressures to conform to the main stream. Even if it may result in death, representing the truth of your Father's kingdom is more important than surrendering to the lying lips of men. Too much may be at stake. By your fortitude, you may be initiating a whole new revival that may take full effect in future times.

The present mindset of your contemporaries may not be able to accommodate such a reform movement of God. You just may be ahead of your time. The spirit of sonship adapts to the lonesomeness of this vocation and continues the work of God unreservedly.

A man clothed in soft raiment living in kings' houses

Having a covering of camel's hair and a daily meal of locusts and wild honey definitely does not assimilate into the lifestyle of palatial living.

This kingly life more absorbs someone who loves to have it easy all of the time, one who loves to be waited on by an array of servants.

Resting on his laurels, this regal mentality accepts all of the credits as others do the work. He loves to bask in the limelight, at the expense of an entourage of overworked assistants.

Living in the king's house is the easy life, with rose petals as your bed and private jets as your main mode of transportation.

But what if God called you to work in the trenches, with no money and no congregation to start with in support? What if God called you to leave the comforts of your ten thousand member ministry and go into a place that has none of the amenities of running water and electricity, and your potential congregation are people who do not possess a high school education? What would you do? If you respond in the negative, then you love the soft clothes, palatial lifestyle and having this soft mentality would disqualify you from operating in the will of God.

John's clothing and diet fit into the role in which God called him to serve. The desert certainly would not have supported the softness and easy-all-the time mentality of religion.

There are some ministerial callings that are not easy by nature. They require a toughness that matches the adverse conditions one may have to face. These adversities include supreme levels of unbelief and stony, unbendable hearts. The son of God quite supernaturally digs deep into the resources of his sonship to withstand the attrition of the *wilderness* calling.

As we have seen, operating with the spirit of a son sets you apart from the ordinary. With boldness like Moses, creativity like David, and the mental toughness of John the Baptist, you evolve at a level that places you beyond the mainstream, church-only *spirituality*. The direct line of communication you continually maintain, through your being, with the dictates from heaven, sets you apart from the mundane, fearful experience of typical Christianity. In the spirit of sonship your every step is in synchronization with the Holy Spirit. The Spirit of God is your only guide, making you a unique individual not infected by the orthodoxy of religion and the conventional controls of social acceptance.

As a son of God you supernaturally flow in the characteristics and personality of the Creator. In the spirit of sonship you are well qualified to represent the Father.

THREE

The Emergence of the SON

The gracious, loving and benevolent character of our Creator has always been revealed from the beginning. His Fatherhood is clear from all of the creative activity recorded in Genesis chapter one.

The fact that an eternal entity who does not require any other entity to exist, brought into being an entirely new existence, which is different in nature to His own, exhibits His love and compassion.

Almighty God's purpose is to create and formulate a spiritual entity that would manage and administer the resources of this physical realm, through the agency, nature and character of His Spirit.

To do this, He would develop mankind, even though they possess a physical component of dust, to be directed to function, as spirit beings, in His image and likeness and therefore, will operate as sons of God on the earth.

To create oneness that exemplifies God's nature, He would send His Son, as Jesus Christ, to be the Head of a body, consisting of a gathering of the sons of God, all knitted together through the Spirit of sonship. This one body would be called SON, prophetically declared in Exodus 4:23 and Psalm 2: 7 and revealed in Hebrews 1:2.

Therefore, the fact that Jesus the Christ came into the territory of mortal man to die for the sins of the world is not the entirety of the Gospel of the Bible. In actuality, the sacrificial blood that was shed on a hill in Calvary was the means which made the reality of the Gospel possible to all men.

This phenomenal event, which will always be the greatest act of love, was a critical part of a process which Almighty God had prearranged from the beginning of time and was pronounced as Divine Will upon all existence (Genesis 1 :26).

This in no way lessens the impact that the death of Jesus has had on the eternal prospects of humanity. Without this single act of selflessness, it would have been impossible for man to escape the bondage of sin. By HIS death, the Father's plan for mankind's development would have indeed become feasible and in fact the Calvary experience was the only means by which man would come to experience Godliness.

> "And I will put enmity between thee and the woman, and between thy seed and *her seed; it shall bruise thy head*, and thou shalt bruise his heel."
>
> Genesis 3:15 (Emphasis added)

To prepare the world for the legitimacy of the earthly rulership of the SON, Almighty God reserved a line of HIS servants which would climax in the *seed of the woman* reestablishing the sovereign rule of heavenly principles. To accomplish such an all-important feat this *seed* must meet the following criteria:

He must be a son of God. Unlike Adam, this seed must have an unbreakable connection to the Command Center of heaven.

He must be a son of man. Like Adam, this seed must walk among the creation to feel and experience its pain, despondency, and sense of hopelessness. Also the creation must be able to see and feel the Deliverer to experience a sense of closeness to Him.

As a son of man, the seed would be in complete agreement with God's law of dominion (Genesis 1: 26). Since God cannot break His own principles, all actions, with respect to the earth, must be performed in the form of man.

From birth to death, this seed must be sinless which would give Him the spiritual right to prepare man for his eternal role of dominion.

Through the Holy Spirit, this seed must be in constant contact with the Ancient of Days. This Godly seed must live in accordance with the Father/son intimacy knowing that HE represents the name of the Father, at all times.

As we peruse the annals of history looking for a possible candidate who can fit all of the above criteria, only one man satisfied all of the conditions: Jesus the Christ.

All of the alleged enlightened men who have claimed to be sent for the elevation of mankind have all failed miserably in meeting each criterion. Mohammed, Confucius, all of the Vatican popes, Gautama Buddha, and Socrates who have all been born out of a union of flesh and blood, nullified their qualification of the condition of sinlessness. Did Jesus fill all of the criteria? Let's see:

Jesus is undoubtedly the Son of God: "While he yet spake, behold, a bright cloud overshadowed them, and behold a voice out of the cloud, which said, This is my beloved son, in whom I am well pleased; hear he him." Matthew 17:5.

Jesus was a son of man. Those who followed Him touched and saw Him in the flesh: "That which was from the beginning, which we have heard, which we have seen with our eyes, which we have looked upon, and our hands have handled, of the Word of life;" 1 John 1:1.

Jesus came into this world through the virgin damsel, Mary who was impregnated by the Holy Ghost. Her betrothed husband to be, Joseph never knew her in any intimate way: "Now the birth of Jesus Christ was on this wise: When as his mother Mary was espoused to Joseph, before they came together, she was found with child of the Holy Ghost." Matthew 1:18.

By this means, the curse of sin was not transferred to Him, at birth and therefore through His 33 years, Jesus never committed a single act of sin.

Jesus led HIS life by the guidance of the Holy Spirit which put Him in intimate contact with the dictates of heaven: "Then was Jesus led up of the spirit into the wilderness to be tempted of the devil." Matthew 4:1.

The great hallmark of Jesus' earthly ministry is the preeminence that HE gave to the Father. Jesus never failed to demonstrate this fact as every opportunity arose: "Ye have heard how I said unto you, I go away, and come again unto you: "If ye loved me, ye would rejoice, because I said, I go unto the Father: for my father is greater than I." John 14:28.

As Jesus met all of the required criteria, there is no doubt that HE was the promised Messiah, the Lamb of God who came into the world to save mankind from the damning effects of sin (John1:29). The evidence from the word of God, in support of this convincing claim, clearly shows the submissive relationship HE employed and the oneness He enjoyed with HIS Father:

> "Then cried Jesus in the temple as he taught, saying, Ye both know me, and ye whence I am: and I am not come of myself, but he that sent me is true, who you know not."
>
> John 7:28-29

> "My Father, which gave them me, is greater than all; and no man is able to pluck them out of my Father's hand. I and my Father are one."
>
> John 10:29-30

> "Then said Jesus unto them, When ye have lifted up the Son of man, then shall ye know that I am he, and that I do nothing of myself; but as my Father hath taught me, I speak these things. And he that sent me is with me; the Father hath not left me alone; for I do always those things that please him."
>
> John 8:28-29

As the true **seed** of the woman (Genesis 3:15) Jesus' sacrifice at Calvary broke the authority and stronghold the enemy had on mankind (bruise thy head) and by HIS death (bruise his heel) the debt created by mankind's allegiance to sinful ways was repaid in full. Man was now free, without any condemnation, to take up his place in the body of the SON, as sons of God.

For those who confess and believe the sacrifice, (and conduct their lives thereby), Jesus had made would have their past sins and iniquities erased and thus withdrawing any hindrance to the coming of the indwelling Holy Spirit.

Before the Father's plan of the perfecting of the SON could take effect, the internal nature of mankind had to be sanitized by Divine control.

Man was under the influence of the evil one and in that respect, he did not have the ability to free himself from the controlling effects of darkness.

This is the reason why the Only Begotten Son of God, had to come to the earth. As purity of spirit, The Christ earned the spiritual right to wrest control of the devil since throughout his tenure, as a son of man, He never at no time gave in to the kingdom of darkness.

Now, the ability to assume divine-like status is passed on to man and his participation in the SON is now assured, as preordained by the Creator.

This is the great news that all of creation was waiting for four thousand years: the appearance of the sons of God on the earth. This is indeed the Gospel that Jesus announced to the world: Sonship is translated to the sons of men, great news indeed. Jesus' death and subsequent resurrection had made it all possible by the cleansing of our inward parts and thereby justifying the impartation of the Holy Ghost and in so doing validating the power of the kingdom of God on the earth.

As John the Baptist and Jesus Christ made their respective declarations: (Matthew 3:1-3) and (Mark 1:14-15), it signified a shift in power from the kingdom of darkness, which had crippled the world for four thousand years since Adam and Eve, to the kingdom of Heaven, through the stewardship of the sons of God.

Through a process of sanctification, the only begotten Son of God, Jesus the Christ, came on earth to initiate the formation of and to be the Head of the spiritually united body of the SON. As this body (the gathering of all the sons of God on the earth) must be developed in agreement with the Divine principles of its Head (Jesus Christ), it must have as its foundation the spirit of sonship.

IN HIM FACTOR

For many centuries, believers have been following Jesus Christ in accordance with Matthew 4:19..."And he said unto them, Follow me, and I will make you fishers of men." To further solidify this position, the term Christian has been given the connotation "Follower of Christ."

What Jesus had in mind, as he spoke to Simon and his brother, Andrew was to have them commit themselves intimately to him so much that their mentality, spirit, and lifestyle would be radically transformed from the life they knew. Instead of casting nets to catch fish, they would now be groomed to participate in transforming the lives of humanity. Their souls would be so reconfigured to facilitate this new, exclusive and single-minded purpose for their lives.

The height and spirit of Jesus' intention has been lost to many over the centuries, which has led to people religiously following Jesus in a detached and superficial way. There is no real commitment to the principles of kingdom of God. Alternatively, believers have devoted themselves more to following the doctrines of their respective denominations.

In this way, believers follow from a *distance*, which creates a psychological fear of total allegiance to the ways of Almighty God. They talk the language but do not follow through with walking in the lifestyle of a son of God.

You must be born again, truly transformed from the former self. This self is deeply rooted in a carnal nature that is in total enmity against the Spirit. Therefore, to be assimilated into the body of Christ there must be a complete denial of this former life coupled with absolute submission to the Spirit of the Son.

Living through self-awareness leads to self-exaltation. In this regard, the carnal nature battles and connives in continuous warfare against any submission to Spirit. A worldly way of life and a religious system of pseudo-worship have been propagated by the carnal self to maintain its importance in the lives of humanity. But as mankind lives in this way, any relationship with Divinity becomes deficient and thereafter, the intimacy necessary is diminished.

Submission to the carnal nature poisons your relationship with the Spirit of Truth. Attending church services, under this anti-God nature, does not legitimize any religious stance, nor can it replace the oneness between Father and son.

Self-awareness truncated the closeness Adam and Eve experienced, with the Creator, in the Garden of Eden and subsequently, thereafter, human beings have struggled to relate to Almighty God, in a way that is based on His holiness.

The submission to Himself that Jesus offers to all of mankind cancels the detriment of Adam and Eve's capitulation to the carnal nature and perfectly offers the solution to mankind's spiritual deficiency.

This is the sacrifice that is mandatory to become one with Christ.... Matthew 10:34-39. The carnal nature would rebel and conjure multiple ways to stay in control. Thus it is necessary to deny yourself and therefore lose your former life.

Holding on to your life....your thoughts, will, desires, and the custom of relying on earthly logic, is to constrict the flow of the Spirit in transforming you into a new creation. A renewed spirit-being must emerge in total sameness with the Head of the body, the Son of God.

This is the essence of the IN HIM factor that accommodates this unison as the Spirit of sonship fuses all into one. To step out of this divine assimilation, by the utilization of your ideas and actions, is to enter into the futility of a religious non-relationship. *YOU* must die and consequently a spiritual son of God arises, walking in the divine power and authority that comes from having eternal life.

In perfect unity with the Father and the Holy Spirit, the Son of God preexisted all things, (Colossians 1:17, 19), so that there is no nature that can withstand the transforming factor IN HIM. As every nature submits to HIM, there must be renewal to the divine nature of Son.

There has been a recent trend by many preachers to disseminate and promote a motivational-type gospel. It has now become the norm to encourage believers to '*be the best you can be*'. Also, '*rise to the top by being the best you*'. This system of teaching is erroneous as it upholds the elevation of the carnal nature. By misusing the word of God to promote self-advancement is playing right into the hands of evil to keep the focus on the innate abilities of humanity and not on the exclusivity of the Spirit.

To utilize the teachings of Jesus Christ in order to claim that *our* understanding and wisdom must be increased has resulted in mankind being plummeted further into the gross darkness of humanism.

Our understanding, mind, intelligence, and will must be totally annihilated so that the mind of Christ should be the only factor by which we operate. The best you can be may appear to be more sophisticated and erudite but it is still *self* masking its uselessness with respect to the ways of the Spirit.

The essence of Jesus' command could be further clarified by his teachings in John 15:4: "Abide in me, and I in you. As the branch cannot bear fruit of itself, except it abide in the vine; no more can ye, except ye abide in me."

The fruit of Godliness could only be exhibited in the lives of the sons of God, as they continually abide in the body of Christ. The sons of God never step outside of the body of the Son. Therefore to follow Jesus takes on a higher meaning than the mediocre practice of the past two thousand years.

> "Father, I will that they also, whom thou hast given me, be with me where I am, that they may behold my glory, which thou hast given me, for thou lovedst me before the foundation of the world."
>
> John 17:24.

This is the only way we can be where HE is, thus forming ONE Body, the SON of God. We must submit all to Him. In this way, we will share (behold) His glory, as fellow sons of God.

Ultimately, at a universal level, Jesus came on the earth to establish ONE ENTITY, ONE SON, with Him being the Head of that body (Colossians 1:18).

If this body does not act in accordance with the will of the mind of Christ, the result would be a disjointed backward movement with the Head one way and the body pulling in different directions: a chaotic situation that could only end in destruction. This is exactly what has occurred over the last two thousand years with the disunited and arrogant believers having different levels of commitment and allegiances.

The *legs* of the body said they were Pentecostals and walked in accordance with that understanding. The *arms* declared they were Jehovah Witnesses and refused to go where the legs were going. The *chest* thought he was the most important part of the body and therefore chided the rest of the body to look towards Rome and the Vatican for spiritual upliftment, forgetting that was the true purpose of the Head, Jesus Christ.

This is the disunity that the Son Of God came on the earth to terminate, setting the band of togetherness and knitting all into one.

The Head of the body is the Son of God, Jesus Christ, therefore the rest of that body must be sons of God, as well, in order to form a powerful, symbiotic entity in total unison and with the understanding that the *legs* are no more important than the *arms*. The *fingers* and the *knees* are equal as also the *chest* and the *belly*.

This is the Body that Jesus came to gather together, one which can accurately represent the glory and superiority of heaven, one which truly accomplishes unity as we are all sons of God, operating and connected by the same spirit of sonship. The IN HIM FACTOR makes it all possible as the same Spirit diffuses throughout the body thus connecting each part with the heart and mind of the Head, the Son Of God.

Jesus the Christ came to make this integration possible and viable, putting mankind in touch with his divine purpose, destiny, and power and reconnecting man to his original glorious future.

> "And lo a voice from heaven, saying, This is my beloved Son, in whom I am well pleased."
>
> Matthew 3:17

This points to the critical nature of the IN HIM FACTOR as discussed previously. God sees only one Son, spiritually. It is our individualistic nature that recognizes separation of spirit, but the holistic and universal God relates to the oneness and sameness of spirit that comes from an amalgamation of Son/sons. This is why God referred to a nation of over one million people as son, in the singular. (Exodus 4:22-23).

In the spirit of sonship

> "And it came to pass, when Jesus had ended these sayings, the people were astonished at his doctrine: For he taught them as one having authority, and not as the scribes."
>
> Matthew 7:28-29

Even in the state of flesh, Jesus knew where He came from. He knew that as the Word of God, He had preeminence over all flesh, so that in the superiority of spirit, He maintained this authority in the realm of the sons of men.

In the spirit of sonship, Jesus took command over every situation that confronted Him. The Son of God exercised His divine authority and power over demonic forces (Matthew 8:28-32) and over every physical impediment (Matthew 9:27-31; 7:20-22; 9:1-8).

In the three and a half years in the public eye, Jesus walked the streets of Palestine with a confidence and boldness that could have only come from an intimacy with God, the Father.

In words and actions, Jesus demonstrated the type of dominion over all flesh which was invested in man from the beginning.

As Adam gave up this divine right of rulership and had severed contact with the intimacy of Divinity, mankind, thereafter, had lost this capacity to take divine charge over spiritual as well physical attacks. Humanity has operated with fear and intimidation when faced with the molestation that comes from the unknown or the unseen.

Mankind operates with timidity which is most evident in religious circles. As with the scribes in Jesus' time, the power to speak with authority, with authenticating and conclusive results, has eluded the practitioners of religion.

Religion, in general, does not give you the power to live without any intimidation because it constantly reminds you of your imperfect state and keeps you in bondage through the consciousness of sin.

The fear that you may sin robs the believer of truly living by the freedom that come in Christ. Every move is saddled in doubt, and thus the believer remains in a docile state, afraid to make any bold moves for the advancement of the kingdom of God.

The contemporary religious church is failing its members in their quest to live victorious lives and many are victims of chronic sicknesses, diseases and exhibit defeat in so many aspects in their walk with God.

Jesus came to restore this sonship spirit and put man in touch with his original function and destiny. With man, operating in the spirit of sonship dominion, the Creator could now look upon His greatest creation, the SON, and say "It is good" (Genesis 1: 4; 10; 12; 18; 21; 25).

Son of Man

Jesus, the Christ is the only begotten Son of God. He was not created as a baby in a manger, at the turn of the first century. HE is Spirit who preceded everything in the physical (John1:2). HE participated in the creation of the universe and in fact Jesus is the reason for the creation of the material world (Colossians 1:16-17). By HIS Spirit all of creation was and will be.

Jesus, the Son existed with God, the Father in a time that is too advanced for human reasoning. But this Jesus, being the incarnate Word of God assumed a fleshly form and came to the world of men with a mission of eternal proportions and divine dimensions to reset and reestablish divine order, through the administration of the SON, to a creation that had shifted out of heavenly alignment.

> "Then saith he unto them, MY soul is exceeding sorrowful, even unto death: tarry ye here, and watch with me. And he went a little further, and fell on his face, and prayed, saying, O my Father, if it be possible, let this cup pass from me: nevertheless not as I will, but as thou wilt."
>
> Matthew 26:38-39

It is difficult for man to fully comprehend what was involved for the purity of Spirit to take on such an immaculate undertaking by assuming a flesh man and mingling in a worldly environment that was in absolute contrast to the nature of heaven. There is nothing in all human experience which could give us an accurate insight into what Jesus endured during HIS tenure on earth.

Whatever was involved it almost caused Jesus to withdraw from this immeasurable assignment as the full weight of HIS mission wrested upon HIS soul, in the garden of Gethsemane. But in the spirit of sonship Jesus submitted to the will of HIS Father, in spite of the gravity of the situation.

Without HIS submission, Jesus knew that mankind would have been held in a state of hopelessness, for all times, the bondage of sin would have continued to hold man in captivity. Therefore with this responsibility, the Son Of God was prepared to endure the excruciating expectancy of sin that HE was about to embrace, by becoming a son of man.

By assuming the likeness of man, the Son of God was accepting the curse of sin, upon Himself, so that humankind could be free to relate to a holy God (Galatians 3:13).

What other hope was there for man. A prisoner cannot free himself except that he serves his full time. Humanity was under an eternal sentence and it would have taken someone who experienced the temptations of living, as a man, to pardon mankind from such hopeless circumstances.

Jesus, the son of man, executed His earthy ministry with supreme sufficiency, leaving no room for the enemy to have power over the sons of God.

In addition, the Creator's plan to delegate dominion to man, over the earth, was in focus. To function in this capacity, man must live in the image and likeness of his Creator. How could this be accomplished when man had made the choice to function in the image and likeness of his carnal self? At the same time, God could not have violated Himself by a direct intervention into the terrestrial region, since this was man's domain.

The Son of God, as a son of man, satisfied all righteous conditions and the laws of Godliness were never broken.

Now the sons of men can become sons of God and function as the Creator willed, with respect to the earth and all of creation.

The formation and the utility of the one body of the SON is well on course.

The greatest event in the history of the world is the coming of the Christ to the earth. With HIS presence among men, HE taught and demonstrated the Fatherly nature of Almighty God. HE expounded on the fact that we can be born again as sons of God, our true identity, putting the kingdom of God within our hearts.

By HIS death, the authority of the enemy is broken and the keys of life and death are aptly returned to the King and His fellow kings.

The power of sin is destroyed in the lives of every man who recognizes Him by faith and thereby bringing *peace* between mankind and Almighty God. The barrier of alienation between God and man is forever broken by HIS sacrifice and intercession.

By HIS resurrection, the power of death is conquered by every son of God and most importantly, the spirit of the sonship of man would be translated to the sons of men, giving us our true connection to the Most High God.

It was always the plan of the Creator to send His Son so that the body of the SON can emerge and through the process of time be perfected to take its rightful place as the head of all creation.

It is for this reason, the Spirit communicates with every soul, urging and directing lives to submit to the Source of all existence. Guiding our lives away from darkness that is dedicated to oppose all the dictates of Heaven and to beguile mankind to pledge his allegiance to the ways of evil.

At the beginning, in the Garden; for the whole duration of humanity's civilization; and at the end, when Jesus returns, the Creator wins. God's plan for man succeeded, even when Adam and his wife yielded to darkness.

Satan's plan for mankind is defeated. His kingdom of Babylon is fallen, even now, and the sons of men are transformed into sons of God.

FOUR

In the Image of the Son

"And he is before all things, and by him all things consist."

Colossians 1:17

It was preordained by the eternal Father that all of creation would emerge out of the Spirit of the Son. The underlying factor that gave rise to created existence originated with a supreme Spirit that preexisted all things.

In the eternal wisdom of the all-powerful God, creation was vested in the image of the Son and thereby this spirit of sonship fundamentally defined the spiritual legitimacy of all structures, institutions, and activities within the created realms of the physical universe and the domain of the spirit.

This gave all created entities a *life* that flowed in a supernatural alignment with the nature of Divinity. There was a spiritual connection that formulated a unison that made all existence, whether in the spirit or in the physical, in essence, one entity, a created whole that accommodated no separation or division of independently-driven parts. There was a divine order that was predicated by the integrative nature of the spirit of the Son.

What defines the nature of reality is its underlying spirit and by this token, all life, in the mind of the Creator, was a reflection of the holiness of HIS character.

In an immeasurable period of time, before the foundation of the earth was laid, Father, Son, and Holy Spirit co-existed in a way that transcends human understanding. Within this period, the will and purpose for creation was preplanned to revolve around the Son.

In order to have and maintain a legal spiritual status, all actions, reactions, and relationships must come under the influence and operate in the Spirit of Christ. On the earth, this Spirit could only come through the activities of the sons of God and in this respect every entity that functions outside of sonship exists in a state of falsehood and is bogus in regard to the will of God.

With the capitulation of Adam and Eve, the presiding spirit that controlled the hearts of men was anti-Heaven and flowed counter to the principles of Almighty God's righteous ways.

As exemplified by the construction of the Tower of Babel, this Babylonian spirit was a conspiracy hatched within the evil corridors in the spiritual realm and implanted within the minds of men to curtail the return of the spirit of sonship.

It is almost unknown, by mankind, that religion is a by-product of this evil plan and was a deliberate insertion to turn hearts away from living through the direct inspiration of Almighty God. So that, over the centuries, the worship, praise, and prayer, through religious means, has had negligible impact in the throne of God and actually plummeted the realm of mankind into a deeper darkness.

Irrespective of how many times the name of Jesus is shouted; no matter how many times the name of God is uttered, without the control of the Spirit of the Son, the work of the body is destined for eternal annihilation.

> "For whom he did foreknow, he also did predestinate to be conformed to the image of his Son, that he might be the firstborn among many brethren."
>
> Romans 8:29

It is in the spirit of sonship that the image of the Son is enveloped. A true representation of all the power, omniscience, righteousness, grace and love is fully invested in the Son.

In the trueness of the image of the Son, all things must fall in line with the laws of Divinity and exist in a state of equilibrium that upholds Godly purpose and destiny.

The Son is the spiritual Head of all creation but the spiritually-evil conspiracy has miniaturized the effectiveness of mankind's existence by creating a religious imagery surrounding the Son.

Building crèches of Nativity, which focuses on a helpless baby lying in a manger, has lessened the power of Christ in the lives of believers. The worldwide distribution of portraits of Jesus, with a likeness, which has no basis in truth, has done nothing to strengthen the resolve of the believer to serve in spirit and in truth. Idols of a body nailed to a cross, which supposedly depict Jesus, has not led to the emergence of a powerful saint on fire for Godly principles. In actually, these icons are sublimely imbedded in an imagery of paganism rather than in the all-powerful First fruit of creation.

Making signs of the cross and praying to statues of Jesus and Mary, in the spirit of religion, has never been anywhere close to the image of the Alpha and the Omega of all life. By the will of the Father, all life, which was initiated through the Son, must validly continue through the Son and evolve to a greater level, after His second coming.

In the image of the Son, creation exercises its greatest potential to reflect the omnipotence of its Creator, Almighty God. The light of God is embedded in every flower, in every blade of grass, in the fruit of every tree, so long as the spirit of the Son is proliferated via the activities of the sons of God, on the earth.

The Son is the light of the world and by divine integration, the presence of the sons of God counters the darkness of any pretentious spirit that sets itself against the unity of the SON.

Every invention is conceived in the spirit of the inventor. The car operated according to the concept within the mind of Mr. Karl Benz, but, over the years, it took engineers, who understood what Mr. Benz had in mind, to upgrade the performance and appearance of the automobile.

In the same way, it will only be through the sons, who are connected to the mind of Christ (1 Corinthians 2:14), that creation would continue to be upgraded, in accordance with the nature of the Son.

Every structure that does not assimilate into the image of the Son will die, as the Son is the Author of life (Colossians 1:16).

The image of the Son which is the same as the image of God (Colossians 1:15), is one that is immersed in eternal power and sovereignty. The power of the Son receives its potency from His connection to the Omnipresence, Omnipotence and Omniscience of the Creator. As spirit begot spirit, the Son emerged out of the Father and therefore in essence, they are the same in every aspect: in nature, character, and spirit (John 10:30).

Nothing could possibly overcome this Divine configuration. No entity could resist the power of the heavenly image, forever. Unless Divinity allows resistance to exist in order to fulfill some purpose, for a specified period, no darkness could legitimately exalt itself over the light of the image of the Son.

Keeping this sovereign power in focus, it becomes obvious that the weaknesses of all religions are not an accurate reflection of the awesomeness of Divinity. No religion, inclusive of Christianity, operates in the supremacy of Divine imagery. They do not recognize the true power of the Son and therefore disqualify themselves from functioning under the potency of the Creator. If they do not recognize the power of the Son, then they cannot identify the inherent command of the sons and in effect do not know that the power of sonship is within their grasp.

The resultant institution is therefore fragile and devoid of any real power to change times and discern seasons and therefore the power to transform mentalities and redundant mindsets is beyond its portfolio.

In the image of the Son, seasonal upgrades in the spirit are recognized and adhered to. There is a constant movement upwards, in attitude, to be on a level of perfection with the Father. Christianity in particular indicts itself as the attempt to perfect its work has not been truly undertaken, through the right spirit, for two thousand years.

> "Moreover whom he did predestinate, them he also called; and whom he called, them he also justified; and whom he justified, them he also glorified."
>
> Romans 8:30

Through the foreknowledge of Almighty God, all things are the result of a divine orchestration predestined to adhere to the preeminence of the SON. From birth, a script has been prewritten for every soul, who has been called, which considered all relationships: our parents, siblings, friends, all of our interactions, were so designed to create a son of God with a personality and character that conformed to the only begotten Son of God. In accordance with our calling as sons, the environments, teachers, and every influence strategically placed in our paths, have been carefully pre-organized with a precision that can only be accomplished in ascendancy of the Spirit.

The sum total of all our experiences should result in conformity to sonship which justifies our lives according to the superiority of the image of the Son and glorifies our Creator through the submission to divine will.

It is for this reason no son of God cowers in fear when faced with any trial or tribulation. He knows that in accordance to his calling, the Father remains in control and that all things work together for his ultimate destiny (Romans 8:28).

Every hardship is so designed to mold and shape our character so that we can be united by the same Spirit which creates the image of the SON. In the end, we gladly embrace all tribulations for the sake of righteousness, as we know that even before the earth came into being all these devices were pre-arranged to squeeze out any hindering spirit that opposes our sonship.

Ultimately, our souls must come on line with the Spirit of the Son so that our nature would be a true reflection of the nature of the Ultimate SON.

At present, creation does not bring any glorification to its Creator, as the body of believers conducts its activities under a spirit of religion. The earth groans under the weight of this counterfeit entity and must be released to express its worship in reverence to the one and only true God.

Through the application of the spirit of sonship, the nature of the SON would regain control over all things and thus the spirit of separation would be amended between Creator and creation.

FIVE

The Kingdom is Ours

In order to maintain a holy atmosphere that would envelope HIS creation, it was so ordained by a spiritual God to have a representative physically present among the trees, cattle and all the beasts of the earth and the seas.

A representative who was so connected to the Source that the original intent and nature of all things would continue to exist and develop according to the Spirit of the Creator. A representative who would govern and take care of every living thing on the earth as if Almighty God Himself was literally present among the creation. This representative would have to be so attached to God that all decisions made and all actions taken would be the same decisions and actions that the Creator would initiate.

In times past, every earthly emperor or king would send specially selected governors to rule conquered territory on behalf of the throne, so that the character, nature and spirit of that kingdom could be imbued into the minds of the conquered peoples.

It was the sole purpose of the governor to ensure that the culture which characterized the mother/fatherland became so ingrained into the collective soul of the conquered inhabitants that they should have perceived themselves not as indigenous people but transformed members of the ruling kingdom.

Conquerors like Alexander the Great, Nebuchadnezzar, and

especially all of the roman Caesars would send their envoys to keep the kingdom ideal alive and growing through the hearts of the new citizens.

In modern times, Democracies would send ambassadors to represent the views of their presidents and prime ministers so that the sovereignty of the individual nations would be preserved. Consequently all citizens of these nations who live in foreign lands could enjoy protection and security via the establishment of embassies, since in diplomatic circles, an embassy is considered a state within a state. As in the natural, so in the spiritual.

In the eternal wisdom of the Godhead, the preordained decision was enunciated, in the Command Center of divine kingdom rule, to establish a governor who would represent Divinity totally, in a physical earth:

> "And God said, Let us make man *in our image, after our likeness;* and let them have *dominion* over the fish of the sea, and over the fowl of the air, and over the cattle, and over all the earth, and over every creeping thing that creepeth upon the earth."
>
> Genesis 1:26 (Emphasis added)

It follows that these governors of the kingdom of God could only legitimately exercise their divine dominion as they function in the image and likeness of the Godhead. In this way the culture of heaven is assuredly transferred and maintained in the physical realm as the specially selected emissaries flow and operate in the same nature as the Source.

The question remains...who are these selected emissaries? ....

> "And Simon Peter answered and said, thou art the Christ, the Son of the living God. And Jesus answered and said unto him, Blessed art thou, Simon Barjona: for flesh and blood hath not revealed it unto thee, but my Father which is in heaven. And I say also unto thee, That thou art Peter, and upon this rock I will build my church; and the gates of hell shall not prevail against it. And I will give unto thee the keys of the kingdom of heaven: and whatsoever thou shalt bind on earth shall be

bound in heaven: and whatsoever thou shall loose on earth shall be loosed in heaven."

Matthew 16:16-19

As the revelation came to Simon Peter as to the true identity of Jesus, being the Son of God, Jesus took the opportunity to reveal the nature of the body which would administer the activities of the kingdom of heaven on the earth.

The rock that Jesus referred to in verse 18 was not Peter personally, as some religions have suggested, but was the principle of sonship by which HIS church would be established and sustained.

The Church or SON which is the unified government designated to supervise the affairs of the kingdom of God on earth, is the collective heart and mind of the Head, Jesus and the sons of God. Jesus, being the ultimate Son, would commission HIS brothers, in collaboration with Himself, to continue the work which HE initiated in the physical region, after HIS ascension to the heavenly domain.

As the keys of the kingdom (the power and the authority) are entrusted to the sons, it follows that the citizenry of the kingdom of God is the solitary body of the SON.

No other created entity would be given this auspicious entitlement, only the sons of God would be given access to all that the kingdom contains: the power, the benefits and every birthright that is derived from living in the presence of God.

As sons of God on the earth, the kingdom is ours. We are the designated spirit beings that are empowered to impact upon the physical territory and are the only true representatives of our awesome Father.

This is a crucial point as it is only through the activities of the kingdom of God, under the administration of the sons, that all of creation would be cradled and nursed in the spirit of sonship. This would guarantee that the physical realm continues to exist as it was created to be: under the holy culture of the Command Center.

If creation is allowed to surrender to another spirit, then the repressive symptoms of hurricanes, earthquakes, and tsunamis would signal a creation's rebellion against the gross darkness that would captivate its supernatural flow in the spirit of the sons of God.

As the commissioning must come from the Command Center, all religions entities, including Christianity, have been invalidated from partaking in the activities of the heavenly kingdom. As sons of God, who have sacrificed their own lives to the Spirit, are the only legal entities entitled to the greatest benefit of being partakers of the nature of Divinity. As sons of the MOST HIGH, we have been elevated to be joint-heirs with Christ:

> "And if children, then heirs; heirs of God, and joint-heirs with Christ; if so be that we suffer with him, that we may be also glorified together."
>
> Romans 8:17

What is the kingdom of God? The kingdom of God is the spiritual environment, culture and atmosphere created by the unequivocal and sovereign presence of Almighty God.

Wherever the presence of God is the atmosphere thus created must be in alignment with the nature and spirit of Divinity. Everything that falls within the kingdom environment must be impacted upon by HIS presence and come under a divine orientation and agreement.

As the kingdom of God is deposited on the inside (Luke 17:21), thereby transforming and reconfiguring our inner beings, wherever we go, we, as divine sons, bring the presence of God to bear upon the physical environment.

This is an important distinction. It means, the sons are more than the citizenry of the kingdom of God, they form part of the make-up of that kingdom. The kingdom is not something you enter but is something you, as a son of God become and thereafter be. The kingdom, on the earth, therefore is the presence of the SON, thus developing.

This is why whatever you bind or loose on earth is bound or loosed in heaven. The SON has dominion on earth, and therefore, his authority to manage the resources of the physical realm, is fully endorsed by heaven, because the presence of the kingdom, on the earth, is spiritually legal and righteous, through the sons only.

This is significant because if we are to be grafted into the body of the SON then we must operate under the same principles, standards, and spirit of the Son of God.

Our cultural expressions based on personality and character must come under heavenly orientation because it is through the heart and mind of the SON, the kingdom of God will be proliferated in the realm of humanity.

As the power of the kingdom of God is within us, the sons of God, it means that wherever we go, divine light, wisdom, purpose and destiny is imparted to our surroundings. Wherever we are the atmosphere of that environment must be altered to reflect the will of God.

Whether it is within our neighborhoods or our workplaces, the sons of God are the light that represents all the supremacy that Heaven is.

In this regard the sons of God are empowered to exercise their authority as ambassadors of the King, through the following ways:

Our internal nature is changed

> "Therefore if any man be in Christ, he is a new creature; old things are passed away; behold, all things are become new."
>
> 2 Corinthians 5:17

As sons of God that make up the kingdom we have been transformed by the nature of the King's Spirit. No longer are we swiveling victims of past circumstances, unable to rise above the fluctuations of life but have been elevated to live by the superiority of spirit over the flesh.

As we are planted in the midst of the worldly system, the deceitfulness of the earthly spirit cannot not have any impact on our souls. As ambassadors of the kingdom of God, our nature, character and culture are diametrically opposite to our designated territory. The razzle-dazzle of this world cannot be attractive to us. Our kingdom responsibilities, duties and work can therefore proceed unhindered, without any distraction from the falsehood of the earthly system.

Power over the physical

> "Verily I say unto you, Whatsoever ye shall bind on earth shall be bound in heaven: and whatsoever ye shall loose on earth shall be loosed in heaven."
>
> Matthew 18:18

As spirit beings, sons of God are not bound by the limitations of earthly time, space and distance. The impediments posed by the laws of physics cannot adversely affect our work in the physical realm. We have the power to reside in the unseen world and thereby deal directly with demonic activities that manifest as imbalances in this material world.

All of our activities are not directed towards fleshly indicators but recognizing these as mere symptoms, *kingdomites* impose their dominance over opposing forces that originate in the spirit.

We have the authority, as the kingdom citizenry, to speak eternal supremacy, to situations, in the spirit, that cause physical distortions and try to impede the forward momentum of the kingdom of God.

By the ascendency of the Kingdom, and being an integral part of, the sons of God can wield the governance that is automatically delivered to them because, with no difference in nature, the King can trust His kings with all the power that is vested in Him; Matthew 28:10.

Kings and Priests

"But ye are a chosen generation, a royal priesthood, an holy nation, a peculiar people; that ye should shew forth the praises of him who hath called you out of darkness into his marvellous light."

1 Peter 2: 9

Translated from darkness and brought into the light of the SON, the sons of God are well positioned to speak to creation, on behalf of the Creator. Imbued with a priest/king nature, the sons of God are *gods* on this terrestrial level of existence.

With the authority of kings, the sons are well poised to assume dominion leadership in guiding, directing and causing creation to be enveloped in an aura of righteousness.

With a Godly interconnection, through their priesthood, the sons are the legitimate oracles, who speak, through prayer, to manifest the spiritual requisites of Almighty God's design, for the earthly realm.

The Father of all creation is dependent on His sons taking up this dual role of representation, and therefore would not operate with respect to earthly affairs, without utilizing a son. Noah, Moses, and ultimately Jesus, all fit into this role, well. The sons of God, in these last days, are perfectly positioned in the body of the SON, to execute the will of their God, precisely and to bring all existence under the ambit of its Creator, for all time.

Human beings cannot function in this dual role. Hence, history is replete with atrocities and abuses, as Church and State have tried to govern as a single entity. It is only through the aegis of the kingdom of God that man is empowered to accomplish the task of bringing creation to rest, as a king/priest, with divine proficiency.

The intelligence of Divinity

"For who has known the mind of the Lord, that he may instruct him? But we have the mind of Christ."

1 Corinthians 2: 16

With all of the marvelous inventions that bring comfort, ease and convenience. With all of the advancements in medical science that prolong our lifespans and with all of the upgrades in computer and electronic technology, mankind believes his intelligence is all that he needs to solve all of the earth's problem that we face.

He believes that in time, with all the knowledge accumulated, over the centuries, would serve as a savior, bringing life on earth to an idyllic state.

But with all the scientific breakthroughs and with all the knowledge attained it is evident that mankind cannot achieve the utopian ideal, by his own effort.

We can attempt to clone human life in a laboratory but we cannot comprehend the inner working of the human brain.

We are capable of sending equipment to Mars, thirty-three million miles away to see if life could be sustained on that planet but we cannot fix the earthly problems of world pollution, the depletion of the ozone layer and global warming.

With all the upgrades in farming techniques and cultivating

methods, we still are nowhere close to feeding every man, woman and child on the planet, on a daily basis.

It is self-evident that our intelligence and wisdom is not enough in dealing with global chronic issues that we ourselves have created. There is no doubt the **Intelligence** that created a perfect universe is way beyond anything mankind can conjure up in his limited and finite mind.

Life on earth needs a divine intelligence to reclaim the beauty and perfection creation was designed to be. Through the interconnecting link of the kingdom of God, this supreme intelligence becomes an integral part of the make-up of the sons of God.

With this birthright, kingdom people operate at a level that belie their natural existence and upbringing. We exist at a supernatural level and experience dispensing wisdom to all aspects of our kingdom lives.

With the mind of the King, we can dissect situations with a clarity that is not shrouded in the density of carnality. We can analyze issues we face and make decisions based on the supremacy of the Spirit.

Where others stumble and falter using the wisdom of this world, we excel in the Source of a wisdom that can discern thoughts that are yet to be formulated because they reside in the future. The Source of intelligence that we are integrated with is not stymied by time or space. It transcends the three-dimensional but in itself is dimensionless and cannot be measured by any known means.

With the power of the kingdom, we could reverse the downward spiral of the world by overcoming the spirit of this material system and applying an intelligence that the world could only admire but is incapable of discerning.

> "I am the door; by me if any man enter in, he shall be saved,
> and shall go in and out, and find pasture."

> John 10:9

Jesus the Christ is the only means by which we can enter into the kingdom of God. HE is the catalyst who makes it possible for us to be grafted into the body of the SON and thereby be partakers of what the kingdom of God is.

There is no other door, other than Jesus by which we can enter. Not religion, not mysticism, not any New Age movement and for sure not Christianity.

Jesus is the only one whose sacrifice of death and thereby repaying the debt caused by sin, gives us the justification to become and live as sons of God and restore the sonship ideal to the earth.

But Jesus was also inferring that HE was the DOOR to gain access to the kingdom. But so many believers stop at the door, not proceeding further into the greatness of what the full presence provides. They live their spiritual lives admiring the door, at the entryway, and therefore cannot exhibit the power and genius that lies beyond.

The DOOR should be admired and reverenced for this is our LORD. But Jesus Himself wants us to experience and participate in the richness of the kingdom: living in the resurrected power and representing His kingdom in the fullness thereof, as its agents in the world. This is the only way we can be seated in heavenly places, in Christ.

Even though the cross provided the means by which we are saved, it is a symbol of shame which Jesus, the Christ took upon Himself so that humanity does not have to experience living with the resultant condemnation and guilt that stems from alienation from our Creator.

Jesus wants us to move on from the shame of the cross and take hold of all the opportunities HIS resurrection makes accessible to us.

Thus, as sons of the MOST HIGH, the kingdom of God is ours to have, to become and to be.

SIX

CHAPTER

The Spirit of the SON

> "But ye shall receive power, after that the Holy Ghost is come upon you: and ye shall be witnesses unto me both in Jerusalem, and in Judea, and in Samaria, and unto the uttermost parts of the earth."
>
> Acts 1:8

A highly significant upheaval coming out of the disobedience of Adam and Eve was the displacement of the Holy Spirit from the indwelling, active participation in the development of the souls of mankind. Since then mankind has been an empty shell totally governed by carnal forces and waiting to occupy a spot in the cemetery.

In the absence of the indwelling Holy Spirit to connect man, intimately, to the Command Center, pandemonium, mayhem, and one disaster after another have plagued mankind's existence, in general. Wars, rumors of war, a multiplicity of conflicts have dominated our history books and it seems that man is not satisfied with living in peace with each other.

The absence of this Godly empowerment has turned man into a greedy, shallow, unintelligent creature addicted to destroying himself and everything around him. He seems to imitate some semblance of wisdom but his propensity to ignore any Godly input puts a twist of evil to everything with which he is involved.

The ability to harness the power within the atom was a dream of many scientists since the late 1930's. The idea was to develop nuclear power plants of electricity as an alternative to the use of hydrocarbons. As the know-how became available, the first use of the technology was the development of the atom bomb which was utilized in the destruction of the Japanese cities of Hiroshima and Nagasaki, in 1945. The first nuclear power plant was designed in 1952. With his twisted mind, void of any righteousness, man's initial instinct is to create something of evil intent.

Of course, man has been able to achieve great accomplishments through many beneficial creations and inventions that have contributed to the improvement of the quality of life.

But I dare say all of these benefits which raise our standard of living have been due to inspiration coming from Heaven. Even though man has turned his back on heavenly principles, the Creator, through HIS amazingly gracious nature, has continued to motivate men to greatness. Most of us are not aware of this grace and so we take credit for wisdom that really belongs to God.

At the beginning of the first century, Almighty God sent HIS Son, Jesus Christ to take away the stumbling block of sin in mankind so that the Holy Spirit could come to the earth as an indwelling and dominant presence.

With the first apostles, sonship is restored; the kingdom of God is about to be proliferated through the hearts of new converts and the Holy Ghost is about to do incredible supernatural works via the Church of Jesus Christ. The development of the SON had begun to take shape.

It is easy to understand that the wisdom and intelligence of the carnal mind is incapable of making any impact upon the realm of the spirit. It would be like a one-celled amoeba of a diameter of 0.028 inches trying to understand the dynamics of the Milky Way of a diameter of 100,000 light years (one light year would be the distance light would cover traveling at a speed of 186, 000 miles every second, in one year, making the diameter of our solar system 186,000*60*60*24*365*100,000 miles).

Even this analogy does not do justice to highlight the difference in nature of the spirit and the natural. There is simply no comparison to give us a full comprehension of the magnitude of the world of the spirit.

Left on his own, without spiritual aid, mankind would be completely annihilated by spiritual evil.

Man's feeble attempt to depict the relevant activity of God is like using third-dimensional vocabulary to describe realities that are beyond the formation of any kind of dimension. Holy writ pens in Isaiah 55:9: "For as the Heavens are higher than the earth, so are my ways higher than your ways, and my thoughts than your thoughts."

How can he come up against an enemy he cannot even see? How can he resist the power of the spirit world with the fragility of his carnal mind? For man to function in the middle of a spiritual reality, he must be empowered through the full control of the Holy Ghost. By this means man is transformed into a spirit being. Even though he has a physical body, man can now participate in the reality of spiritual activity. He can prophesy the word of God and cause his environment to change. He can be in contact with the Command Center and receive valid instructions in the performance of his duties.

There is no doubt the presence of the Holy Spirit is crucial to the creation of the son of God and to the forward movement of the kingdom of God on this earth. Without this holy impact, the kingdom would slow down as it did with religion and the spirit of sonship would not be the dominant force in the region of the earth.

Then, man would resort to the darkness of his religious activities cutting off all contact with heaven. The Holy Spirit is the currency that stimulates the economy of the kingdom of God, in the sphere of the physical. He functions in several capacities. The Spirit of the spirit of sonship is in service to the sons of God in the following ways:

HE defines our sonship

> "For as many as are led by the Spirit of God, they are the sons of God"

> Romans 8:14

In order to live and function as a son of God, the Holy Spirit must not only dwell in us, HE must be given access to actively engage our souls. It's not enough to be blessed by the promise of God (Joel 2:28-29), but if we do not allow the Spirit to control our insides, continuously, then we continue to be sons of the flesh.

A son of God and the Holy Spirit are inseparable. It is HE who legitimizes our sonship. Without Him we would be like salt which has lost its saltiness (Mark 9:50).

The Spirit of holiness remains our constant companion, always guiding, urging, empowering and convicting our lives.

AS HE dwells within us, there is no distance between us and Heaven, which could be used by our enemies to negatively influence our thinking. He couldn't be any closer, creating an intimate bonding, which places us at a higher level than any other created being. Not even the angels have this privilege. HE is close enough to effectively transform our nature.

HE defines the culture of the kingdom of God

> "For the kingdom of God is not meat and drink; but righteousness, peace, and joy in the Holy Ghost."
>
> Romans 14:17

The nature of each kingdom is influential on the lifestyles of all its citizens: the thought processes, the speech patterns, the dress code and the general behavioral models have all taken shape as a consequence of the spirit of the kingdom. In general, the culture of each domain is a manifestation of the nature and character of the ruling spirit.

Every kingdom that has ever existed has received its identity from the nature of its monarch. If the king/queen was evil then the kingdom would go down in posterity as an evil one.

The kingdom culture thus developed was a reflection of the nature and character of its ruler. The Elizabethan Age of stability and prosperity in the history of Great Britain was instigated by the ruler of the era: Queen Elizabeth 1, (Nov.1558 - Mar.1603), whose matriarchal personality influenced the spirit of the era. As a contrast, the years between 1509 and 1547 would always be known as a dark period in British history as the king, Henry V111 ruled as a tyrant, killing all of his opponents by the most atrocious means. Known for his massive ego and super-inflated self-esteem he wielded his authoritative rule, giving the era its notorious reputation.

The spiritual kingdom of God is enveloped in an atmosphere of righteousness, peace and joy, all of which are given by the presence of the Holy Ghost. The righteousness of the kingdom sets it apart from anything man could ever hope to emulate.

Under the righteous culture of the kingdom, each citizen is guaranteed equality of treatment and status: (Romans 2:11). Not so in the circles of religion where a hierarchy is erected so that the Clergy could lord it over the Laity.

Under the righteousness of God's rule, there is equity of the application of each law and regulation to each citizen. The various laws, precepts are inherently righteous and were created to develop and encourage righteous living among the citizenry, without exception.

Not so with many of the earthly kingdoms of the past. Distribution of the kingdom's resources was not done equally. It was done as a good gesture of the monarch and not as a right of each citizen. Many laws, as practiced by these earthly kingdoms, were unjust which was an indication of the nature and thereby the culture of each particular kingdom and the nature of their kings/queens.

The peace and joy of the kingdom of God makes it a unique entity. No system that man has ever created has instilled a sense of inner contentment and peace. We have been subjected to the flippant nature of mankind's personality. But with the culture that comes from above, its unchanging disposition gives us a confidence to trust in Almighty God's presence, in the midst of the variations of this material world.

The kingdom of God, which is not about meat and drink, (the acquisition and accumulation of material wealth), does not encourage its citizens to focus on the effervescence of materialism (Matthew 6:25-32) but on the presence of the King who can change your cultural expectations in accordance with the ways of righteousness:

> "But seek ye first the kingdom of God, and his righteousness;
> and all these things shall be added unto you."

Matthew 6:33

HE transforms our orthodox thinking and breaks our dependence on tradition

"And be not conformed to this world; but be ye transformed by the renewing of your mind, that ye may prove what is that good, and acceptable, and perfect, will of God."

Romans 12:2

As we receive the redemptive work of Jesus, in our hearts, the Holy Spirit takes up residence within us and transforms our thinking to reflect our new status as sons of God.

The Holy Spirit is ever present to guide us away from mankind's propensity to go back to the orthodoxy and familiarity of past religious doctrines.

As with the apostle Peter who allowed his Judaic upbringing to cloud his sonship judgment, he had to be vividly informed by a Holy Ghost vision so that the demands of the kingdom could be met at that time (Acts 10).

So many of us fall into the trap of returning to the useless vomit of Pentecostalism, Christianity, Lutheranism, etc., as we have developed the habit of relying on regular patterns of doing things.

We live in a contrived culture that supports the repetitions of actions by the majority which brings comfort and confidence to our frail eyes. But the ways of the kingdom are not the ways of the world (John 18:36).

It is the work of the Holy Spirit to release our minds sullied by the bondage set by worldly traditions, religious entrapments, and the falsehood of self-conscious pseudo-spiritual activity to the infinity of the mind of Christ.

The Holy Spirit wants the believer in this 21st century to release himself from the infancy of the praise, prayer, and worship of the 20th century. The Holy Spirit wants to reform our myopic view of God and release us into a higher level of knowledge of the Father.

The church has become too orthodox, afraid to be taken into new ways of lifestyle worship because they look strange to the human mind. Absolute trust in unknown circumstances is not what the Church live by so rather than embrace the Spirit to upgrade, the believers prefer to play it safe and stay within the strict parameters of traditional religion.

But if Peter had played it safe then Cornelius and his gentile generation would have stayed outside the will of God, never receiving the gift of the Holy Spirit and would have continued to worship what they did not understand (Acts 10).

If the apostle, Paul had played it safe, then he would have never ventured to Rome and would have ended his days in obscurity (Acts 21: 11-14).

The Church has been engaged in ways of worship which have not changed for decades. We must break free from our fear of being branded as different by the Pharisaical spirit which has dampened the progress of the Church, within the last two thousand years.

The believers need to be upgraded to a greater level of spiritual awareness so that we can accurately function in the season of sonship, in these last days.

It is the job of the Holy Spirit to sanitize our hearts so that the spiritual truths of times to come could be accommodated.

HE makes us holy

Not wearing any jewelry, wearing your dress down to ankle length, discarding all of your make-up and covering up your hair all day do not make you holy. It is not about the flesh, it is about the presence of the Holy Spirit working on the hardness of your heart.

Once you allow the Holy Spirit access to your soul then you would be guided into all truth.

Your behavior, lifestyle, and thinking, will all fall into alignment with the holiness of the kingdom, but to achieve holiness through the adherence of your religious do's and don'ts would not make you any holier than the unbeliever (Isaiah 64:6).

Holiness is a quality that only comes from the presence of the Spirit. There is nothing we can do to become holy, except to give in to HIS authority. Our do's and don'ts are opinions shaped by our denominational standing which do not reflect the holiness that comes from God. It's not about clothes but about the condition of your heart. If it was so then Adam and Eve would have been right to put on clothes of fig leaves.

It's not about make up but in the spirit and attitude of your internal self. You can wear the longest dress or choose not to put on your wedding ring but if your heart is tainted with unforgiveness or you lack mercy for your enemy then you would have no part in the kingdom of God. It's all about the Holy Spirit and allowing HIM all of who you are.

HE is a comforter

> "And I will pray the Father, and he shall give you another Comforter, that he may abide with you forever."
>
> John 14:16

In the three and a half years the apostles walked with Jesus as they ministered the gospel, they had developed an amazing comradeship with their Master. He was everything to them: teacher, confidant, and friend.

Now that HE was intimating to them that HE was about to leave, they felt a sorrow that only comes from the death of a loved one. HE was a comforter to them. HIS presence brought feelings of security, peace, and a sense that all will be well. As long as Jesus was present, the human fears that come from not knowing what the future holds did not arise.

As if HE sensed their apprehensions at His departure, He allayed their fears by indicating that another Comforter just like Him would arrive to take HIS place.

This Comforter, the Holy Ghost, would go further and illuminate every issue Jesus spoke to them about that was cloudy to them.

This new companion would open up their hearts to a whole new world of understanding and enlightenment. Further to this, the coming Holy Spirit would empower them to do greater works (John 14:12).

This is the role of the Holy Spirit. HE brings comfort by teaching us about things that our innate intelligence cannot process. HE brings comfort by giving us a sense of belonging. HIS internal presence gives us a connection to Almighty God. We do not feel all alone in this universe: defenseless and abandoned. HE brings comfort by confirming to our inner beings our continued existence when our bodies return to dust. He gives us the assurance of eternal life.

A true Comforter and friend, HIS presence imparts a joy that cannot be sourced through any other entity.

As the Holy Spirit testifies to us about the Son of God, HE fills a void in our lives that makes us feel predestined to be a major part of the dynamics of the universal SON.

HE opens our eyes to a greater understanding of the Word of God

> "I have fed you with milk, and not meat; for hitherto ye were not able to bear it, neither yet now are ye able."
>
> 1 Corinthians 3:2

The word of God, the Bible, is an inexhaustible source of spiritual experiences and an ever progressing height of spiritual power. For those who think that they have heard it all before and that in the last century the fullness of scripture had been delivered, should rethink this position.

Scripture is a spiritual entity that operates on so many levels all at the same time that it becomes virtually impossible for the human mind to contain a fraction of its truth (1 Corinthians 13: 9-12).

This is the work of the Holy One who integrates with our true selves and downloads spiritual truths to the collective mind of the body, eliminating the use of the superficial carnal mind. The Holy Spirit raises us to an intelligence, on a level of God-like understanding.

This acquired knowledge of divine quality does not operate in a vacuum only to impress others with our wealth of knowledge. There is a transformation that occurs and an evolving practicality about God's word that affects our lifestyles and guides our daily walk according to Godly ways.

Besides, it is more than knowing things and the ability to recite memorized scripture. The word of God is Spirit that is *food* for perfecting our souls. The word of God is the only medication that can solve any sickness that affects the soul.

As our understanding of the fullest use of the Word, as elucidated by the Holy Spirit, becomes clear to us, we become a living word of God; breathing, walking, talking scripture where people can be positively affected as they 'read' our lifestyles.

HE empowers us to hear the voice of God

"He that is of God heareth God's words: ye therefore hear them not, because ye are not of God."

John 8:47

Almighty God speaks. He speaks in audible tones that enable human ears to hear, as with Moses on Mt. Sinai (Exodus 19:19). He also speaks in inaudible tones which only the Spirit can decipher (Revelation 1:10). In both cases it is the workings of the Holy Spirit which give us the ability to hear when the Absolute speaks.

In the first scenario, where HIS voice is rendered audible, without the enablement of the Spirit, HIS voice would come across as thunder. You would know that you heard something but would not be able to decode the source of that communication (John 12:29). In the second scenario, the Spirit opens your spiritual ears to collect the spiritual data and translate it into information. Without the activation of your spiritual ears, you are denigrated to rely on your religious traditions as orated by your pastor/priest. This is an unacceptable arrangement, for any error made by the leader would be taken as gospel by the hearer and without the ability to verify the message, the erroneous teachings are destined to be disseminated unchallenged.

Jesus said "My sheep hear my voice", (John 10:27), which implies that if you cannot understand and therefore be obedient to the voice of the King then you are not spiritually connected. You have not submitted to the Holy Spirit and you are not part of the kingdom of God.

It's impossible for the written word to aptly convey all the fullness of God's truth. The earthy- formulated languages of men are too limited to hold all that God is and therefore it is most critical to yield to the holy indwelling presence so that the accuracy of your understanding would not be shrouded in doubt and suspicion.

The Rhema word of God is significant to our work in the kingdom, and our ability to hear and be obedient to Him is even more critical to our sonship.

"He that hath ears to hear, let him hear."

Matthew 11:15

The work of the Holy Spirit is no doubt crucial to the sons of God who constitute the Church of Jesus Christ. Without HIS prominence, the keys of the kingdom, as mandated by the King, would not be adequately administered in the earthly realm.

The Holy Spirit ensures that through the spirit of sonship the movement is kept in line with the culture of Heaven and that no leaven of religious theology is kneaded into the kingdom process (Luke 12:1).

Ever since the Church has been relocated to Rome there has been a concerted effort by the forces of darkness to stall the kingdom of God by depersonalizing the Holy Spirit and restricting HIS control by man-made inventions and the worldly socialization of church life. But as the sons of God begin to reassert their position in this 21st century, through the ascendancy of the SON the preeminence of the Holy Spirit would rise to supreme levels, once again.

SEVEN

CHAPTER

The Spirit of Emancipation

In the Gospel of St. John, chapter five, verses one through nine, the story is released to us about the emancipation of an impotent man who was incapacitated for thirty-eight years, both mentally and physically.

In a condition of dependency, the infirmed man could not rise above his mental state of inertia. He had resigned himself to a defeated life, whereby his inactivated mind, which was anesthetized by thirty-eight years of immobility, could not search for alternative solutions to his problem.

Instead of waiting for the movement of an angel, the man should have known that he needed to stop depending on a method that didn't work for so many years and rethink his position by taking a radical departure from the norm.

He should have tried a radical approach but his mind, which was asleep for most of his adult life, couldn't be elevated because of the resident spirit of disability, hesitation, resignation, and defeat.

Jesus had to come and inject life into the deadness of the man's situation. By activating a spirit of release, Jesus recognized that the man needed a mental renewal and therefore wanted to extract a positive response as the Son of God asked the question "Wilt thou be made whole?" (v6). But the man's negativity was indicative of his mental incapacity.

In that context, Jesus had to release the Word of life "Rise, take up thy bed, and walk" (v8), transforming the man's life and unlocking the prison cell of his spirit.

From its inception in Rome, in the early years of the first century, until this day, the Christian church has exhibited the same mentality as the impotent man at the pool.

Waiting for something to happen, most believers have sunk into a state of dependency, overburdening their leaders to continually pray for them. The typical believer of today has accepted his position of weakness, thinking that he is not worthy to achieve anything great and to receive the best of anything.

So the church-goers are always on the look out to receive a blessing from their pastors, while they sit back and procrastinate. They are always in attendance at every prophetic meeting hoping that the prophet would single them out for a special mention, so that their deflated self-esteem could receive a boost. They are always on the hunt to witness signs and wonders with the expectation that some magic may rub off on their sterile spiritual lives.

The so-called church is in effect a hospital, full of casualties waiting for angels to come and stir the stagnated waters in their minds. This spirit of dependency has imprisoned most church-goers, placing them in a spiritual and mental prison of their own making. A religious mindset which has been inculcated into the believers, for many centuries, has been deliberately designed to prevent them from rising out of the ashes of their infertile past.

Afraid to step out into the innovation of the Holy Spirit, they prefer to stay within the narrow confines of their denominational traditions. Like the Jews in the story, who put more focus on their Sabbath law and not in the triumph of light over darkness in the man's life, the typical Christian would rather stay in an inactive state. Buried in a grave of do's and don'ts they would shy away from releasing themselves to the creativity of the Spirit.

Through this means, the believer has become a weak victim of circumstances, always looking for a shoulder to cry on. He does not want to go through any adversity, at no time. If so, he looks to blame everyone from God to the pastor for his troubles.

How far has the contemporary church come from the fortitude of the first century church as they considered it an honor to suffer for Christ?

The church of today exists in a state of bondage. Owing to the fear of stepping out into unfamiliar territory, the contemporary body of believers has screeched to a standstill choosing instead to rely on past outdated methods.

But as a new season of spirituality approaches, the old forerunners would make themselves irrelevant as they persist with the old redundant ways. The old religious spirit has imported into the church a tendency to be timid, uncreative, and fearful of newness.

There is an attitude that finds full expression in 'this is the way it has been done for years and this is the way it's going to stay'.

This spirit is stifling the church. The worship, praise and prayer have become repetitious and ordinary. The various religious fellowships have become crippled by this mental ineptitude.

The result? An imprisonment that blocks the way forward; a fear that prevents the believer from severing and discarding the umbilical cord of overdependence on the church leadership; a low self-esteem that nourishes a sense of unworthiness in the hearts of the practitioners; and a bondage that inhibits the freedom in relating to Almighty God beyond conventional means. The uninhibited worship in the Holy Ghost has been cramped by pride and self-consciousness.

Will thou be made whole?

The same question posed to the impotent man by the Son of God, is presently directed to the present-day church.

Sitting by the pool of inactivity, in a condition of religious repression, the church must respond in the positive in order to become more effective in this new season of liberty.

The spirit of sonship releases a freedom that can break the mentalities of impotence, infirmity and religious imprisonment.

There is no limit to Spirit nor can the Spirit be restricted. The Spirit will continue to upgrade in accordance with the necessary requirements as a new season shifts into high gear.

In the timeless spirit of sonship, the minds of the believers are emancipated from all man-made and pseudo-spiritual structures.

Every repressed spirit that has been inhibited by denominational ritualism is released fully to reconnect with the Spirit of freedom.

In the power of the spirit of sonship the atmosphere of any environment is electrified, bringing about a transformation from spiritual inertness and inadequacy to spiritual vibrancy and unlimited capabilities; from Christianity to sonship. Instead of a sterile believer bearing no fruit for the kingdom of God, the sonship spirit recreates a fearless, passionate warrior for Christ unshackled from the incapacitating chains of religious impotency.

By the spirit of sonship, a freedom from all self- expressions is discharged to the believer to reverence and revel in a tehila-like worship with no consideration for who's looking on or who disapproves of your unconventional methods. The intimacy between the Father and the son takes precedence over everything else. You are totally unrestricted to worship in truth.

Rise, take up thy bed and walk

This is a call for every believer to step out of their spiritual slumber and live in the newness of the Spirit. As you release yourself to the Spirit of the Son, the old attitude of warming the benches every Sunday service only to receive is reformed by the zealousness to make your contribution to the kingdom process.

You become an asset always willing to impart a blessing for the sake of Christ. You no longer become a burden to the fellowship but a worthy advocate, always willing to assist in whatever capacity. You clean the pews, the washrooms, and perform usher duties with sincere joy.

As expansive as the universe is, it cannot contain an iota of the vastness of Almighty God. Nothing in all existence can hold the limitless nature of the Creator and in this regard, the Spirit, which operates in the same *infiniteness*, cannot be contained by the folly of our religious parameters. In trying to control the Spirit with our mundane rites and ceremonies, we run the risk of being disoriented with seasonal upgrades.

This is a critical issue as the Spirit demands that fruit is produced in harmony with the excellence of the coming season.

Just like the fig tree in Jesus' time failed to satisfy the high demands of Divinity to produce, (Mark 11:12-14), every entity which pretends to be part of the flow of the Spirit but cannot bring forth the right kind of results would be discarded for its uselessness.

In these end times there is a challenge placed on every institution to flow in oneness with the Spirit. It is only spirit that can keep up with Spirit so that as you flow through the spirit of sonship you are well positioned and equipped to fulfill the requirements to produce appropriate fruit and contribute to the advancement of divine cause in the earthly realm.

One of the major effects of the Son of God, Jesus' presence among the sons of men was the release of the Word of liberation to the enslaved minds and hearts of the Jewish nation.

In the preceding two-thousand year period, before the advent of the Messiah, the people of God had degenerated into a state of spiritual bondage, just like the unholy nations that surrounded them.

They had misinterpreted the Laws of Moses and missed the spiritual flavor which was embedded in all the statutes and regulations.

Over the centuries they became entrapped by the misuse of the Torah's divine wisdom. The Pharisees, in particular, became the most susceptible to this spirit and because of their stature in Jewish society they managed to infect the whole nation with this deceiving spirit.

As Jesus released the Word, the underlying spirit of emancipation freed many Jews from the many years of estrangement and strangulation, allowing the disciples especially to march forth to the beat of the kingdom's forward movement.

As if history is activated in cycles, the present day church is at the same level of bondage as the Jewish nation in the Messiah's time. The sonship spirit through which the initial apostles operated, had been dampened as the emphasis was placed on the practice of the many religions in existence.

Many of today's Christians would dispute the fact that they have been practicing their beliefs in captivity. But if you do not comprehend the depth of a son of God and think that it is just a title, then you are a slave to religion. If you are afraid to operate in greatness because you suffer with low spiritual self-esteem then the spirit of religion has captured you. If you live by a denominational code at the expense of the guidance of the Holy Spirit then your spiritual growth is stunted and cannot flourish in the prison of your mind.

But the all-embracing spirit of sonship is about to be discharged in an intensity the world has never experienced before. It will emancipate mindsets that have been stalled for centuries. It will release believers from their fear of stepping out of the shadowy existence of traditional religious practices. It will liberate the minds of the saints to embrace and understand a higher level of spiritual consciousness.

As the sons of God begin to execute their spiritual superiority, from the forefront, and in the full view of a global audience, a spirit of emancipation would be released, universally that would transform old redundant doctrinal structures and eliminate various levels of spiritual blindness.

A spirit would be proliferated that would resonate with all sons of God thereby initiating a connection that would lead to the gathering of the brethren. The formation of the Body of the one true Church would be well under way.

The structure of the contemporary church would be altered by the emancipated minds of the twenty-first century sons of God.

EIGHT

CHAPTER

The Gathering of the Brethren

"O Jerusalem, Jerusalem, thou that killest the prophets, and
stonest them which are sent unto thee, how often would I
have gathered thy children together, even as a hen gathereth
her chickens under her wings, and ye would not!"

Matthew 23:37

Out of the loving nature of Divinity, it was always the ultimate purpose
to have all of creation bonded by the same Spirit and thereby develop
without antagonism, estrangement, spiritual separation, and divisiveness.
Almighty God showcased His intention, for all things, by creating the
entity of a single nation, through the faith of one man.

From Abraham, throughout the exploits of the Patriarchs, and up
to the Hebraic experiences in Egypt, the complete development of one
nation was always the focus. When the Jews were finally released from
the harshness of the Egyptian whips and chains, they exited, under the
leadership of Moses, as one united body. The Church in the wilderness,
therefore, was an entire race of people, united in the common cause of
coming face-to-face with their God.

It did not take long for division and in-fighting to bring disruption to
the togetherness that would have characterized them as a special nation,
set aside by God (Exodus 32:26-28). Thereafter, throughout their history,
the desire to wholeheartedly serve Almighty God was always a challenge
and in that regard, the unity which would have been preserved and set

by God, was lost (1 Kings 11: 31-33). The Jews paid the price of ultimate estrangement by betraying their divine legacy, their Deliverer, (1 Samuel 8:5-9), and the universal plan of the Creator.

The divine presence that the nation of the Jews experienced, throughout their history, was not only for them but was a microcosm of a greater design that would encompass all of creation and administered through the integrative SON. Before the beginning of time, the mind of Divinity envisaged a spiritually-collective physical realm in complete balance with the spirit of Heaven.

The Jewish nation was one component of a history-long orchestration that took into consideration and utilized the rebellion of Lucifer, Adam and Eve's submission to darkness, humanity's love for self, and the religious tinkering by the powers of this world. The time of the Gentiles would also be another major component of the plan and in the end, all divergent spirits would be annihilated so that a new creation would emerge, under the influence of the Spirit of the SON. Creator and creation would be intimate. Two shall become one, and Jew and Gentile would love each other and have fellowship, as brethren (Ephesians 3:6).

Jesus' lament, (Matthew 23:37), therefore, is a universal one. It is directed towards a disunited church that has been emasculated by two thousand years of religious tomfoolery. The Pentecostal, Seventh-day Adventist, Roman Catholic, Anglican and so many of today's Religions cannot gather together to form a unitary platform that would challenge the present ascendancy of the carnal world. Their purpose is to prove the validity of their individual beliefs, at all cost. The current so-called church, as a consequence, has become weak and ineffective, not offering much hope with respect to the issues that confront humankind, today.

This is not the legacy which the first century believers has bequeathed to posterity, so that we can advance the forward momentum of the kingdom of God. Then, throughout the regions of Palestine, Asia, and Rome, the sons of God transformed the spiritual topography of every area they traversed. The lives of thousands of Jews and Gentiles alike were impacted upon by the kingdom teachings of Paul, Peter, John and the rest.

What was taught in Jerusalem was also taught in Corinth, Galatia, Ephesus, Philippi, Colossi, Thessalonica, and Rome. What was practiced as a son-of-God lifestyle was no different in any of the assemblies, in any of these territories. Thus, this was one church with many branches, operating with celestial power and vindicated by signs and wonders. This was not many churches operating counter to each other, as it is today.

Therefore, the first-century church truly represented the dictates of Heaven, as every move and thinking came exclusively from the Holy Spirit. They lived as sons of God so that all activities were emerged in the Spirit of sonship, as the Creator willed for the development of His church.

After three centuries of doctrinal interference in Rome, things began to change. The teachings on sonship were gradually phased out and replaced by religious Christianity. The freedom that came in Christ was replaced by the sin-conscious condemnation of denominational laws and regulations. Papal supremacy was inculcated into the minds of generations of new believers and a whole belief system on sainthood took precedence in the lives of millions of Europeans and subsequently, the whole of the western world.

The reactionary creation of multiple religions that came from Martin Luther and others from 1517 and onwards, did not assist in uniting the church. Matters got worse as several churches now fought each other for global supremacy and expansion. For the last two thousand years this situation has been exacerbated by the aloof attitude of religious practitioners as they go to extremes to prove *I, alone am right, everyone else is wrong.* Jesus' lament (Matthew 23:37) reverberates even louder in this twenty-first century.

It is not generally known that the disunity caused was a result of a deliberate strategy by the forces of darkness. Religion was a methodical idea transferred to the minds of humans, by anti-God powers and facilitated by the Elite class of worldly leadership.

> "The kings of the earth set themselves, and the rulers take
> counsel together, against the Lord, and against his anointed,
> Let us break their bands asunder, and cast away their cords
> from us."

> Psalm 2:2-3

The powers of this world know that a disunited church would work to their advantage as no opposition and resistance could come from a weakened entity that has become dependent on surviving through the earthly system of doing things. The *band* of oneness of the church is broken into a multitude of denominational settings and a myriad number of religious spirits.

In contemporary times, there is a movement that is dedicated to bringing together several religions into some form of united arrangement. Leaders from Mecca and Jerusalem have been approached to meet with the Pope in the Vatican, behind closed doors. In the glare of publicity, the proposal has been put forward to unite all of the major religions in a quest to achieve religious tolerance and subsequently, world peace. This is a farce and a continuation of the worldly leadership conspiracy. It is impossible for religion to be united. It is in its divisive nature to keep its individual ascendency, at the expense of everything else. Therefore one wonders if biblical prophecy is unfolding, in the creation of one world religion, (New World Order), before us.

To achieve the unity that characterizes the nature of Divinity, the church must be bonded by the same Spirit of its Head. The universal gathering and spiritual intimacy of the Brethren could only take place through the Son:

> "I will declare the decree: the Lord hath said unto me, thou art my son, this day have I begotten thee. Ask of me, and I shall give thee the heathen for thine inheritance, and the uttermost parts of the earth, for thine possession."
>
> Psalm 2:7-8

This day is upon us as the era of the sons of God is in full motion, encompassing all races of people, of every nation, from the furthest reaches of this earth.

This is the unity that can only be achieved in the Spirit of sonship as it relinks the breaking of the band, as set by the kings of the earth, and knits all into togetherness because the Head of the body is the Son of God. Then as the same Spirit diffuses throughout the body, the *legs* of the body are sons of God. The *fingers* are sons of God. The *chest* and the *belly* are sons of God, as well.

With sameness, no animosity and estrangement could exist, therefore the church is transformed into a powerful entity that is truly the head and not the tail, with no weapon forming against it ever possibly overcoming it. This church is the gathering for which creation is holding its breath: Romans 8:19, as the sons of God put aside all else and sacrifice everything to assume their responsibility of dominion over all terrestrial life: Genesis 1:26.

The rock or foundation of the church is sonship. This is clear from the revelation Peter received, from the Spirit, Matthew 16:13-18. It was revealed, at that time, that Jesus is the Son of God, not a mere prophet or man of God but the incarnate of Divinity and in the light of this He came to duplicate Himself in making many sons of the same spiritual nature: Hebrews 2:10. The sons of God, when gathered together through a global spiritual network, would perfect the work of God and bring creation to rest.

> "For the creature was made subject to vanity, not willingly, but by reason of him who hath subjected the same in hope. Because the creature itself also shall be delivered from the bondage of corruption into the glorious liberty of the children of God. For we know that the whole creation groaneth and travaileth in pain together until now."
>
> Romans 8:20-22

Creation is in dire need of the gathering of the sons of God. Under the weight of the repressive spirit of darkness, creation cannot function as it was meant to so do. Divine dominion was given to the sons (Genesis 1:26), for a reason. With the sons of God in control of this earthly realm, and operating in the image and likeness of the Creator, creation would function and develop through divine order.

Since the religious gathering has lost sight of the sonship ideal, creation is groaning for its release from evil. Not until the network created by the spiritual gathering of the sons of God takes place, and the true church of the Son of God emerges, creation would continue to exhibit signs of suppression.

Would a perfect God allow an imperfect creation to exist forever? Almighty God has been developing His sons, over the centuries, to wrest control of that repressive spirit and through their presence in the body of the perfect SON, creation can experience the freedom that comes from the light of Divine order. Creation would be at rest. "It was good": Genesis1:10, 12, 18, 21, and 25; would materialize as the Creator envisaged it.

Mankind needs the gathering of the sons of God. It is the will of the Creator for His greatest creation –man, to live and function via His image and likeness and therefore represent Him, in the intimacy of a Father and son relationship (Genesis 1:26). Human beings have rejected this divine configuration and instead have chosen to live by their own devices.

As a consequence, humankind does not know how to love each other. We live by a code of self-fulfillment, at the expense of everyone else. Hate, envy, and suspicion characterize a human race that is duped and conditioned by a spirit of *survival of the fittest*.

Instead of the closeness of sonship, humanity has settled for the long-distance pseudo-relationship of religion. In this way, life has been dominated by separation and disunity. Our religious convictions have led to fanaticism and have exposed an intolerance that leads to impiety, a false sense of superiority, and total disrespect.

There is nothing in mankind's history that has stirred up so much division among the human species as religion has managed to accomplish. As it impacts the soul, no other pursuit can agitate passion to extreme heights of which religion is capable.

Our historical records reveal how detrimental religion has been to our relationship with one another. Most of the wars, throughout civilization, have been fought along religious differences. Armed conflicts still dominate news headlines, in the Middle East, as two major religions fight for world recognition. The nation of Pakistan was created, in 1945, as Hindus and Moslems could not live with each other, even though they shared ancestral blood-lines. Northern Ireland has been polarized, over its existence, as Catholics and Protestants cannot see eye-to-eye. Also, history reminds us of the massive amount of innocent blood that was shed during the Christian Crusades of the middle ages between 1096 and 1291 AD and the armed conflicts initiated by the Adherents of Islam, in North Africa in the eleventh century.

In the Spirit of sonship, man was created to be so intimate that the darkness of hate, animosity, and distrust would not control his relationship with others. The term brethren would come to mean a white man embracing a black man, in love; a Jew praying together with a Gentile, in complete fellowship; an entire global race, lifting their collective hand and heart to the one true God.

The Creator has blessed each human soul with the same spiritual deposit, so that as we yield to that spiritual reality, we can be connected and gathered, through the same Spirit, bringing harmony and peace to all existence. The breath of life that enlivened Adam is the same spirit that has been passed down to each of his descendants.

In this regard, essentially, we are all the same, from within. This enables all of humanity to be spiritually connected into one entity, thus facilitating man's position in the completeness of the SON.

It is the carnal ego that recognizes and facilitates separation and individuality. It places the focus on external appearances and consequently, as man struggles to exist in this superficial manner, a whole illusionary system has been created to accommodate and justify living in the flesh. As a distraction, the ego keeps the emphasis on worldly order of things to maintain its dominance over the Spirit.

In the end, the reality of spiritual oneness shapes the purpose and lively hope of mankind's destiny-a future that is driven by the Gathering of the Brethren.

NINE

Praying in the Spirit of Sonship

The popular concept many people have had, over the centuries, concerning prayer is one where we direct our personal petitions to an all-powerful entity who is more than capable of performing miraculous acts on our behalf. The conventional idea directs us towards God to fulfill our needs and wants, whenever it is beyond our capacity to acquire those needs.

People from every level of society, in every civilization, throughout the history of mankind, have held close to their hearts the notion that there is a higher authority who is there to respond to all our whims and fancies. The concept is refined even further by the belief that Divinity rewards us for our devotional acts of faith. The many adherents to the various faiths continue to practice in hope, looking forward to a merited response from Deity.

> "Ask, and it shall be given you, seek, and ye shall find; knock, and it shall be opened unto you: For every one that asketh receiveth: and he that seeketh findeth; and to him that knocketh it shall be opened."
>
> Matthew 7:8

In accordance with the above scripture, mankind has been asking, seeking, and knocking, repetitiously, for all millennia. But this meritocracy ideal mankind has attached to prayer has not brought into consideration the grace of God and has resulted in so many believers falling away. Several unanswered prayers are erroneously justified by a perceived lack of faith and or tenacity.

So many devotees resort to the idea that God does not hear their supplications because either they are not worthy to capture God's attention or they did not pray long enough to impress the supreme Spirit.

These anthropomorphist attributes that mankind has attested to God have always taken us down a wrong path and has contributed towards the distance artificially created, by man, between Divinity and humanity.

> "But when ye pray, use not vain repetitions, as the heathen do: for they think that they shall be heard for their much speaking. Be not ye therefore like unto them: for your Father knoweth what things ye have need of, before ye ask him."
>
> Matthew 6:7-8

The conventional, universally accepted concept of prayer is always perceived from a standpoint of self-gratification. It is about fulfilling the needs of the carnal state. It is about gratifying personal desires of the pray-er. As a contrast, the son of God, who has been created to participate in the highest level of prayer, the focus on self-purpose, does not exist. The son of God zeroes in on his divine purpose, the entire reason for his appearance on the earth and applies his God-driven destiny in the administration of his prayer life.

Closer scrutiny of the scripture mentioned above, makes the notion of bombarding heaven with the tenacity of repetitious prayer, a lie. Verse eight raises questions as to the purpose of praying when the fact exists that our Father already knows what our needs are. Why do we have ask God to supply our needs when HE knows what are those needs better than we do?

It is evident that God requires us to pray (Matthew 6:9) but the self-centered concept of prayer must be brought into question.

> "Therefore take no thought, saying, What shall we eat? Or, What shall we drink? Or Wherewithal shall we be clothed? (For after all these things do the Gentiles seek :) for your

heavenly Father knoweth that ye have need of all these things. But seek ye first the kingdom of God, and his righteousness, and all these things shall be added unto you. Take therefore no thought for the morrow: for the morrow shall take thought for the things of itself. Sufficient unto the day is the evil thereof.

Matthew 6:31-34

For a son of God prayer is not seen as a vehicle to satisfy self and the acquisitions of material needs. He takes his prayer life to a God-like level whereby it is all about fulfilling a divine function. It's all about the dissemination of the ideals, concepts, and spirit of the kingdom of God. As the son is always driven by the Spirit of God, he prays on the basis of the Creator's original assignment for the SON.

The Assignment

"And God said, Let us make man in our image, after our likeness: and let them have dominion over the fish of the sea, and over the fowl of the air, and over the cattle, and over all the earth, and over every creeping thing that creepeth upon the earth."

Genesis 1:26

The son of God is created, as an ambassador of heaven, to dress and keep the earth (Genesis 2:15). The son is charged to ensure that all of God's creatures would continue to develop in the one true Holy Spirit of its Creator. This divine responsibility is predicated on the fact that the son of God is imbued with the characteristics of his God which gives him an intimacy with his Father, at all times. This ensures that the carnal nature of the material does not distract him from his original purpose.

According to the foreknowledge of Divinity, the precursors of this eternal arrangement, Adam and Eve, allowed the Deceiver to reshift their consciousness from God to themselves (Genesis 3:1-6) and as a consequence, an evil influence has blanketed the earth, since then. Mankind, over the centuries, has continued to focus on his outward needs at the expense of creation (his eternal assignment) which has led to the earth being subjected to the darkened bondage of Godlessness:

> "For we know that the whole creation groaneth and travaileth
> in pain together until now."

Romans 8:22

Since man has lost sight of this divine assignment, his prayer has circled around his narrow-minded world: a world where he is the center of all the attention. He expects Almighty God to put the spotlight on him alone, to the deprivation of everything else.

Functioning in the image and likeness of his God, the son revolves his prayer life, selflessly, around his foremost commission and concern. In the spirit of dominion (Genesis 1:26), the son directs his energies towards the conditions of the world; the mental, physical, spiritual, and emotional state of every human being on the planet.

Of concern to the son is the adverse effects industrial and domestic pollution has on the world environment. The son cannot turn a blind eye to global warming and the effects of the green gas phenomena on climatic conditions, with the attitude that these things are not important to him because they do not impact on his tangible needs. Therefore, his prayer turns away from himself and is directed to a Godly intervention and restoration of all creation.

Instead, many believers have concentrated on satisfying their never ending wants, their insatiable desires to please self and their murderous ways to get ahead of everybody else. Conversely, the son knows the earth will continue to rebel if man persists with this destructive tendency (Romans 8:19-21) and so in a devout manner, he sacrifices himself and his personal comfort for the sake of God's creation. All of his prayer is focused on the emergence and manifestation of the sons of God, so that divine order and balance can be interjected into a chaotic system upheld by the religion of self-importance and self-gratification.

It is in the spirit of sonship all of God's sons have prayed throughout the ages. Even those who lived before the coming of the Messiah, Jesus Christ and were temporarily emerged in that spirit, have all kept true to the development of the Father's perfect SON (Jesus Christ: the head of the body and the sons of God: the rest of the body). This has been the Father's plan since the Garden in Eden. This is the **man** spoken of in Genesis 1:26, and Isaiah 66:2, and this is the son prophesied in Exodus 4:23.

The elements of the prayer of a son of God

There is a common thread that runs through all of the prayer of every son of God. There are basic elements that are consistent in each prayer of the sons. To identify these elements, the prayer of Nehemiah, Daniel and Jesus are examined. Even though the lives of Nehemiah, Daniel and Jesus are set at different times and under different circumstances, making their respective tasks different in some ways, each of the three prayer is in alignment with the original assignment (Genesis 1:26). Each prayer enunciates the perfecting of the SON who would have spiritual dominion over all creation, as discussed earlier in this chapter. In this regard, these three sons prayed in like manner (Daniel and Nehemiah were showered in that sonship spirit and Jesus being the only begotten Son).

Nehemiah's prayer: Nehemiah 1:4-11

Daniel's prayer: Daniel 9:1-19

Jesus' prayer: John 17: 1-26

These are the elements of the prayer of a son of God:

1/ The son of God discerns the times and seasons he is activated in and prays accordingly and initiates an appropriate atmospheric activation.

2/ The son of God understands his role as a minority and never allows small numbers to deter or distract him.

3/ The son of God always has a deep concern for humanity, not himself.

4/ The son of God always prays according to the original assignment.

5/ The son of God always sacrifices himself for the greater cause.

6/ The prayer of a son of God is always clothed in humility.

1/

Daniel 9:2 "I Daniel understood by books the numbers of the years"

John 17:1 "Father the hour is come"

The Father places his sons in certain specific seasons of his great master plan. Each son understands his involvement in the season in which he is activated . The Father directs his sons to pronounce declarative decrees into the spiritual atmosphere at the particular time, thereby initiating the execution phases of the divine plan. The son comprehends the role he plays in the fulfillment of God's will and follows through with his responsibility in speaking God's word into being.

In Daniel's case, it was the preset time for the Jews to return to Jerusalem after seventy years of Babylonian captivity. He therefore prayed to activate the spiritual requirements to initiate the return.

In Jesus' case, the final stage of the divine plan was about to unfold. He was about to return to his Father and the kingdom of God was about to be spread abroad from the small beginnings of the mustard seed into a great tree with many branches in the form of the universal body of Christ. This body consists of the Christ as the head and the sons of God as the body. In agreement, Jesus prayed "Glorify the Son."

2/

Nehemiah 1:6 "for the children of Israel"

Daniel 9:11 "all Israel have transgressed thy law"

John 17:4 "I have glorified thy name in the earth"

In Nehemiah's and Daniel's time, one man prayed for an entire nation. Jesus prayed for all of the sons of God, for all the ages. Almighty

God does not require large numbers to pray the sonship prayer. With many people, the likelihood exist that there would be different spirits in operation thereby stunting the pray from being effective.

3/

Nehemiah 1:4 "I sat down and wept, and mourned certain days"

Daniel 9:3 "with fasting, and sackcloth, and ashes."

One striking characteristic of the sonship prayer is the selfless spirit of the supplication. The son sacrifices his personal needs, puts aside his comfort for the sake of others and feels the pain of those in great affliction. Whenever there is any disaster in the world, his heart bleeds for those in distress and prays for the sick and needy. The present state of his livelihood is irrelevant. Even if he is in a state of comfort, the son puts aside himself and identifies with the poor and dispossessed.

Both Nehemiah and Daniel were in the service of their respective kings. That would have meant they would have experienced a higher standard of living than their brethren. They rejected their own security for the sake of God's people who were in dire need of deliverance.

For Jesus, he paid the ultimate price for the sake of the world. He left his glory, as Spirit, to live among the filth and decadence of this worldly system, so that we, the sons of men can live above the power of the carnal state, as sons of God.

4/

John 17:1 "Glorify the Son"

God's plan has always been about the glorification of the SON in the execution of his duties, as custodian of all the earth (Genesis 1:26). The history of civilization has been in actuality a Godly orchestration of events leading to the perfecting of this SON. From Noah to present times, a divine script has been unfolding in specific seasons: Abraham and the Patriarchs; the nation of Israel; the Prophets; the Messiah; the Apostles and the contemporary sons of God have all contributed to the release of spiritual declarations, all coming into alignment with the ultimate will of God.

As an example of this alignment, Daniel's prayer for the nation of God's people to return to Jerusalem is prophetic of all the sons throughout the ages to come out of the worldly system of Babylon and allow the image and likeness of God to exclusively define their lifestyles.

In this present season, all the sons of God must focus their prayer exclusively towards the culmination of the divine plan. The manifestation of the sons should be unfolding in these end times so that the true spirit of creation can shape and influence the entire universe (Romans 8:19).

5/

Nehemiah 1:4 "mourned certain days"

Daniel 9:3 "with fasting and sackcloth and ashes"

It is not burdensome for the son of God to give of himself totally for the greater cause. They deny themselves as a matter of their internal make-up for they know creation is dependent on their self-sacrifice. This is more than the detached intercessory praying, as practiced by certain modern day believers, but it is the absolute dissolution of all self-awareness, in service to ABBA. These are the sacrificial lambs by which others would come to know Jesus Christ as Lord, intimately.

These sons of the Most High consider this duty as one to be joyously embraced, the reason for their being and willingly submit themselves to the cross of self-denial, even unto death.

6/

Nehemiah 1:6 "and confess the sins of the children of Israel which we sinned against thee: both I and my father's house have sinned."

Daniel 9:5 "We have sinned, and have committed iniquity, and have done wickedly, and have rebelled, even by departing from thy precepts and from thy judgments."

John 17:1 "These words spake Jesus, and lifted up his eyes to heaven."

With all the power and authority vested in the son, he always submits himself before the Father, recognizing that the Father is the Source of all Life. He does nothing on his own but only what he sees the Father does. Even the words he speaks proceed out of the mouth of the Father.

His prayer is not from a foundation of aloofness but it flows out of a spirit of servanthood. He sees himself as a conduit of heavenly blessings in order to be a blessing to others. His prayer is truly intercessory, including himself as one no better than his brethren.

We have looked at the pure motive of a son of God's prayer. Now we look at why he has to pray.

It was the original intention of God to have man represent him on the earth, on the basis of the kingdom of heaven. Almighty God not only gave man the responsibility to care for the earth but also the authority to speak on his behalf. This is why God prophetically gave a peek into the future by authorizing Adam to name all the animals:

> "And out of the ground the Lord God formed every beast of the field, and every fowl of the air, and brought them unto Adam to see what he would call them: and whatsoever Adam called every living creature that was the name thereof."
>
> Genesis 2:19

We have already explored the fact that the Creator invested a delegated authority of dominion to His SON with respect to the earth. Since Almighty God would not rescind on this action, the Father will always *depend* on a son to exercise divine will upon the earth.

In this respect, Noah was led to speak to creation, as the adamic season was coming to an end. (2 Peter 2:5). That is why God moved into action, after four hundred years of grievous slavery, when Moses was led to give the command "Let my son go" (Exodus 4:23). That is why God has spoken to all of creation by His Son (Hebrew 1:2).

The Father would not act or create any movement on the earth unless a son of God gives an utterance on behalf of Divinity. The Father has so ordained that the SON is the head of all creation (Colossians1:16) and in this regard, the SON must give the command to initiate all divine actions on this level.

The son of God who is shaped in the image of the Father would only endorse what is in the Father's mind, because the Father and the son are of the same spiritual nature. That is why whatsoever the son binds on earth is bound in heaven and whatsoever he looses on earth is loosed in heaven (Matthew 16:19).

These divine utterances of the son are what are generally regarded as prayer. Under the spirit of dominion, the son of God must speak (pray) in order to execute divine principles on this earth. Whenever the Father is about to make a shift, HE directs a son, through the Holy Spirit, to make decrees. This is clearly seen in Revelation 8:3-5:

> "And another angel came and stood at the altar, having a golden censer, and there was given unto him much incense, that he should offer it with the prayers of all saints upon the golden alter which was before the throne. And the smoke of the incense, which came with *the* prayers of the saints, ascended up before God out of the angel's hand. And the angel took the censer, and filled it with fire of the altar, and cast it into the earth: and there were voices, and thunderings, and lightnings, and an earthquake."

The role of the prayer of the saints (sons) evidently contributes to spiritual changes that take place on the earthly realm. It is clear that the self-centered prayer that is offered today cannot form part in these paradigm-framing phenomena. Additionally, as the emphasis is placed on all of the saints, in the scripture, it follows that every son prays in submission to the same Spirit, all of them being washed in the spirit of dominion, the will of Creator for all of existence.

Even though the son has the privilege to approach the throne of grace and ask anything of his Father, he executes prayer at the highest level of self-sacrifice. There is no recognition of self in his being and fully participates in the proliferation of God's will. His prayer is geared towards creation and the restoration of the spirit of sonship in accordance with the indwelling dominion factor released from heaven. With his personal care and needs, he faithfully places in the hands of his Father (Matthew 6: 26-34) and gladly submits to the role and purpose for which he was created.

TEN

Worshipping in the Spirit of Sonship

Lifting our hands in obeisance to a Supreme Being has been an activity of humanity from his earliest beginnings. Throughout the recorded exploits of every civilization, there is evidence to support that man always looked towards the heavens, in reverence to a higher authority.

Often times, the recipient of worship have always been viewed as a distant, out-of-reach Deity that is beyond the scope, understanding and intelligence of the worshipper.

In an attempt to make sense of all the unknowns and mysteries that challenges his systematic mind, mankind has always searched the skies for answers. He did not create himself and therefore there must be an unreachable force that he is incapable of comprehending.

By faith, mankind continues to shower his praises to unseen Gods in an attempt to solicit some kind of response. His worship thus is an exercise to bring some form of justification to his existence. If his God responds then he would know that all his inadequacies, insecurities and feelings of inferiority would not matter so much.

Then there are some among us who question why a God would require and revel in the worship of inferior beings? As a means of espousing their atheistic views, these people make a mockery of the believer's passion of bowing before an Entity that cannot be seen nor understood.

But there is a God that created the Heaven, heavens and the Earth; a loving and benevolent Creator that is driven by HIS Father-like passion to share HIS nature with all of HIS creation.

The question remains why would the Father of creation require worship from His created beings? In our search for answers, let us attempt to arrive at an appropriate definition of worship, for a son of God.

> *"But the hour cometh*, and now is, when the *true worshippers* shall worship the *Father* in *spirit and in truth*: for the Father seeketh such to worship him. *God is a Spirit*: and they that worship him must worship him in spirit and in truth."
>
> John 4: 23-24 (Emphasis added)

There are certain key words and phrases in Jesus' teaching that require closer scrutiny, in order to extract our definition:

But the hour cometh

Jesus was implying to the Samaritan woman that all the worship offered up to that point was not of the required quality to attract the attention of Heaven. As the woman admitted "Our fathers worshipped in this mountain"....vs 20, mankind has always attributed worship to a specific place. Even today, people of faith believe that worship must be done in their respective churches, as God is ever present in the assembly of the saints.

In this way, people wait until the time of their church services to raise their voices to their God. It is inconceivable for some to enter into any kind of worship in any other public place. That would amount to sacrilege.

Even the Jews practiced their worship in Jerusalem only. But Jesus brought clarity to the issue by taking geography out of the equation:

> Jesus said unto her, Woman, believe me, the hour cometh, when ye shall neither in this mountain, nor yet at Jerusalem, worship the Father."
>
> John 4:21

In addition to the irrelevance of the location of our worship, the woman's statement (verse 20) is typical of the approach many people have with respect to worship. They see it as a ritualistic practice they have adopted from their parents and elders before them.

In that way, worship becomes an impersonal exercise whereby people do what they see other people are doing. It has become conventional and routine.

True Worshippers

There is an implication here that there is a minority who has taken worship to the level which Divinity requires. This remnant of God's children is unconventional and unique and has made worship into a divine and personal encounter.

Father

Worship, then, is an internal and intimate experience between Father and HIS sons. It has nothing to do with your surroundings (although two or more people can worship together) nor is your worship affected by any external factor. It emanates from the deepest recesses of your soul. It is about relating to Almighty God as Father thus eliminating any alienation between Divinity and you.

In spirit and in truth

Your worship must be embedded in the right spirit and motive. It cannot be immersed in a self-motivating attitude, whereby you are trying to appease God through self-centered activities. Worship is developed in the realm of Godly consciousness rather than in the self-realization of humanistic praise.

The Father seeketh

There is a crucial point to be observed here. For centuries, man has worshipped God from his humanistic perspective. The conventional notion of worship which has been passed down through the ages is viewed as man's attempt to reach out to God in reverence and in thanksgiving. But Jesus takes this issue to a diametrically opposite direction. Worship is about what the Father wants and not what man does. Worship, then, revolves in the realm of the Creator and what is HIS will and purpose is for all creation.

God is a Spirit

Worship is a spiritual realization. It is something to be experienced on a spiritual level. It is not a detached carnal mind attempting to search out a distant God, it is God in you communicating and fellowshipping with your spiritual soul. This necessitates the removal and participation of all aspects of self. The Holy Spirit must be allowed to play the only role in your acts of worship (verses 10, 13, 14).

It is also significant that Jesus switched from using the Father and deliberately used the word God. This was to make it clear in the woman's mind that the God who she was trying to relate to was His Father, setting the stage for her eventual transformation and the revelation of who He is. She was proudly holding on to her past, (verses 12 and 20). Jesus was about to change her worship, forever.

Out of the edification of Jesus' teachings on the subject, we can now attempt to give an in-depth definition of worship.

Worship is a divine initiative that impacts upon and defines the life walk of the practitioner, which accentuates the ultimate spiritual union between the Father and His sons and results in the will of the Creator being manifested in the earth.

This is vastly removed from the popular view people have of worship. Conventionally, worship would be defined as an act of reverence poured out to a superior Being in the hope that this Supreme Being would respond, so that some form of justification can be established.

It has already been pointed out in previous chapters, that for a son of God the mundane, superficial and popularly driven acts of the majority cannot capture his imagination. A son is elected to a higher calling. He cannot be satisfied by nor can he succumb to the mediocrity of the conventional. A son of God is a selfless creature that submits all of his actions to the Holy Power and in this regard, everything about his life is initiated from Heaven. The self-motivated activities of Christianity are not pleasing to him.

That is why John, the Baptist was ostracized by his contemporaries for being different. It is in this context, Jesus was misunderstood by the majority of Jews, in his time. It is clearly understood, now, why Paul was not totally trusted by his fellow believers. That is why the prayer and worship of the son of God would never be readily accepted by the religious hierarchy of the day.

But this is what the Father desires and therefore *seeks* out those who are willing to sacrifice their lives for the sake of the Spirit and totally deny self for the advancement of the kingdom of God.

The Creator deposits a spirit of worship and praise into the son so that for the son, worship is a spontaneous response to the will of the Father. Elements of thanksgiving are always embedded in his acts of worship, but for the son, reverential obeisance is a supernatural aspect of his internal make-up.

The Worship of the Son

> And the four beasts had each of them six wings about him; and they were full of eyes within: and they rest not day and night, saying, Holy,holy, holy, Lord God Almighty, which was, and is, and is to come. And when those beasts give glory and honour and thanks to him that sat on the throne, who liveth for ever and ever, The four and twenty elders fall down before him that sat on the throne, and worship him that liveth for ever and ever, and cast their crowns before the throne saying, Thou art worthy, O Lord, to receive glory and honour and power: for thou hast created all things and for thy pleasure they are and were created."
>
> Revelation 4:8-11

The scripture given above best describes worshipping in the spirit of sonship.

For the son of God, worship is an intimacy he experiences every hour of the time he spends on this earth and would continue in that trend for all times.

Singing songs of praise to the Most High, in church, forms a small, initial phase of his worship experience. It is taken to an ultimate level whereby his every footstep is an act of acknowledgement of his heavenly SOURCE.

Everything that he does and says stems from a Godly consciousness and in this respect, all of his thoughts and movements are directed spiritually to accomplish the reason for his appearance in this world.

For further edification we key in certain words strategically placed in the scripture given.

Full of eyes within

The son of God is imbued with the presence of God from within. In this way, his worship is dictated by the Spirit and not by what external circumstances reveal. What he "sees" and "knows" about the Father validates his worship and praise. The wisdom, intelligence and all-knowing qualities of God are part of his internal makeup and therefore he worships what he knows and understands, in all truth (John 4:22).

They rest not day and night.

The worship experience of the son is a continuous encounter with Divinity that never ends. All of his being has been so transfigured to be in constant contact with the Godhead.

Worship then is complete fellowship, with the Spirit, that is never broken, especially outside of the narrow confines of the church. It is constant acknowledgement of God in his day-to-day walk, in the power that emanates from within. His every step is ordered to fulfil a divine function.

At every level, Spirit directs all aspects of the mind and now the worshipper steps out in ecstatic joy to accomplish a predetermined task.

Jesus' encounter with the Samaritan woman at the well is an example of this. Jesus in full worship mode allowed the Spirit to take his mind beyond his physical thirst so that the spiritual thirst for souls could be satisfied. (John 4:6-30).

Another example of sonship worship occurred as a result of Paul and Silas' experience in prison (Acts 16:23-34). Because they redirected their minds from the debilitating sights that confronted their eyes, the process of worship began by singing songs of praise (v25). In spite of the beatings (v 23) and the grievous conditions of the prison (v 24), through their selfless acts of worship, a prison guard and his family experienced the transforming power of God.

Fall down before Him

The place is set for the twenty-four elders to be seated about the throne (Revelation 4:4). Now we see them leaving their positions of honor and falling down before Him.

For the son of God, worship is an action in all humility which is greater than the vociferation of words and songs.

Anyone can say "God is great" but the true worshipper is galvanized into some action which proves that indeed, God is great.

If I may be allowed a personal interjection which brings home the point:

"Before the start of one of our services in the Fellowship, I came in early to do some reading to be followed by a period of praise and worship. I had set aside certain times to accomplish each aspect of my time with God. I felt so strongly about doing this that I determined in my heart nothing would stop me from accomplishing what I set out to do.

I got through the reading very well and was about to enter into the praise hour when I noticed that the window panes were very dusty, to the point where it bothered me. I proceeded to clean the windows quickly, so that I could return to the business at hand. But as soon as I would begin to praise, another pane would appear to be dirtier than the last one.

When I finally got through with all of the windows, I realized that all of the allotted time was gone. I got so upset with myself, I prayed and repented for allowing the devil to distract me from the real reason I was in church.

While sitting there waiting for service to start, I heard the Holy Spirit say "Don't you know that you worshipped."

I said "How"?

And the Holy Spirit replied "By you cleaning the windows, you acknowledged Father more than your words could ever do."

That experience changed my view of worship, forever.

We can shout "Father, I worship you", several times but it's in our active, spirit-driven lifestyles, steeped in a selfless motive, true worship resides.

Cast their crowns before the throne

Throughout this chapter, it has been reiterated that true worship (worship that has been nurtured in the spirit of sonship) has nothing to do with our initiative. Worship is not what we do in order for God to respond. Rather, it is what God initiates and downloads so that the son could respond, accurately and effectively. True worship is not viewed from the human position but from a Godly perspective.

This takes the element of self out of the act of worship making it a divine experience whereby God is given access to our souls. Worship, then, becomes an intimate fellowship with Divinity, on a continuous basis. No carnal issue can therefore short-circuit the worship process in our day-to-day walk in the Spirit.

On the contrary, putting the focus from a standpoint of self, makes worship a cry out to God to respond so that our need to be connected can be satisfied. This implies that there is no permanent connection between God and man and therefore worship is seen as an exercise to bring the two together. As a consequence, worship is not from the inside but is influenced from the outside, carnal nature.

At this level of humanism, worship becomes a vehicle to satisfy our emotional needs and our desire to be certain of God's love. It usually does not lead into any action, so long as the need of self is satisfied.

In contrast, a true worshipper knows that he is always connected and so, like the twenty-four elders, his desire is to submit to the Father's will and to return all honor to the Source. He does not look for any glory but automatically responds to that internal spark that solidifies his eternal communion to the Godhead.

"Thou has created all things and for thy pleasure they are and were created."

In previous chapters, we have seen how it was the Creator's intention to have a permanent, internal and intimate relationship with man, through the SON, His greatest creation. The disconnection that occurred in the Garden in Eden and the resultant disparity between God and man, over the centuries, is well known.

We have also been edified with respect to Almighty God's master plan to reestablish that spiritual link which would reignite the whole of creation's development, in the spirit of sonship.

As the believer participates in the worship experience, a transformation occurs that arrests the influence of the carnal nature. This is the true purpose of worship where the influence of the Spirit can become the dominant force in man's life. As he submits to the Holy Spirit, in an increasing capacity, his real internal nature becomes uppermost in his life. The more he worships, the more the transformation becomes complete.

It has been a long process which began in Noah's time, and which has transcended all of humanity's history and continues to this day. This level of worship must escalate in these end times, in accordance with the Creator's purpose for all things. Then as the SON (the complete body of Christ) is thus perfected, all of creation can worship the Father in the spirit of sonship and in truth. As creation functions in its original purpose, then Creator and creation can truly become ONE.

> "O worship the Lord in the beauty of holiness: fear before him, all the earth."
>
> Psalm 96:9.

ELEVEN

CHAPTER

The Perfection of the SON...The Season of the Manifestation

In an infinite period before the foundations of the planet, earth and the universe were laid, the Creator, Almighty God had a plan to delegate to His SON the headship role of all creation.

He would create spiritual sons who would occupy the region of the earth and would knit these sons together with the First begotten Son, Jesus Christ (Hebrews 1:6).

Jesus would be the Head of the Body and the second begotten sons would form the torso, arms, legs and feet of the Body. This Body would be viewed and related to as the SON, by the Father of all creation.

Since these sons would have a formation of dust as part of their makeup, the Father in His wisdom would strategize a plan to spiritualize their internal nature so that they would form an intimate connection to Heaven and not to the carnal nature of their physical surroundings.

This is crucial in order to have the Entity, SON, operate under the same spirit of sonship. The purity of spirit that Jesus is cannot be closely knitted to any other spirit, less there be any spiritual contamination of the Body.

Operating under the sameness of a divine, celestial spirit, the Body then can fulfill its destiny of rulership of all creation.

So important it is to achieve this oneness that Almighty God has taken all of mankind's history to accomplish this spiritual integration. He has left nothing to chance.

By predestination, Almighty God has been taking man through a cleansing process whereby every iota of darkness would be squeezed out by the history lessons of life.

In His wisdom, God had to take us through these periods of darkness (famine, wars, and religion) so that man would recognize Light and come to embrace Him willingly. God would not force Himself upon mankind but would teach us how to accept godliness out of pure love.

Because of His foreknowledge, God would make use of the rebellion of Lucifer and his army of fallen angels to discipline and guide humanity toward righteousness and holiness. He foreknew that Adam and Eve would have capitulated in the Garden.

He foresaw mankind's insurgence against Godly lifestyles. He even foresaw man's frail attempt of worship, prayer, and spiritual relationship through religious works and therefore He pre-organized His plan to take man through specific stages of development.

It has been a long journey spanning the entirety of mankind's history, but the Father is all-knowing and every aspect of the plan is being worked out with a divine precision. Nothing that has happened has occurred by chance. The Ancient of Days has always been in total control of every aspect of man's activities, directing and orchestrating to a predesigned end.

Even in man's darkest hour, God has been involved in humanity's development. God is love and it has always been His purpose to share with His SON the beauty of creation.

The Father is relatable and has always desired a relationship with all of His created beings. In this respect, He has ordained His SON to have dominion over creation, as the SON is perfected to reflect the total image and likeness of Divinity. All of history has been a sanctification process to arrive at this perfection.

The Head, Jesus the Christ, has always been ready but it is the Body, the sons of God (because of the influence of the carnal nature), has to be taken through this cleansing process.

The process was initiated and set into motion when Abraham was guided away from his idolatrous past. Because of his obedience, Abraham's descendants, the Jewish race, would play a major role in this master plan.

From Abraham, the plan gained momentum through the exploits of the Patriarchs. It is from this juncture that the inhabitants of the surrounding nations began to realize that the True and living God was active in the lives of the sons of men. Isaac, Jacob, and Joseph especially, were all led to show to the world, the power of the Divine when men are set apart by Almighty God.

From the Patriarchs the scope of the plan was elevated through the nation of Israel. By breaking the mighty power of the Egyptians and by the exhibition of myriad miracles, human consciousness was now directed towards the presence of the true Creator. As the nation became settled in the land of promise, as promised, there was no doubt that Almighty God was shaping an entire nation of people to represent Him.

The wood and stone gods of the people of the world could not accomplish all of the unexplained miracles of the Jewish experience. Try as they did, no one could explain the parting of the Red Sea. Not even the scientific methods of today can explain the Jewish phenomena of 1351BC to 1271BC, except by the intervention of Divinity.

Whenever the Israelites became disobedient to the ways of Divinity, the Father would give them over to His enemies, as a means of sculpting the righteous development of the SON.

The Babylonians, Medes and Persians were all used to make a contribution towards the differential of the righteous freedom of light over the bondage of darkness in the overall completion of God's SON.

Everything was now set for the emergence of the SON. It was through this Jewish race that the Messiah would make His appearance to creation, in the form of a son of man.

The redemptive work of Jesus has been adequately covered in a previous chapter, but it is important to state, at this point, that the overall plan took on a global dimension to include all of humanity and evolved from the exclusivity of the Jews.

The inclusion of the Gentiles

From the beginning, Almighty God had always intended to include every race of people that makes up humanity. From Abraham to Jesus, the Jews were the main recipients of Almighty God's attention but the inclusion of the Gentiles was prewritten into the Plan, before the foundation of the Earth.

Even at the time of the Jewish captivity, Almighty God touched the hearts of the kings Nebuchadnezzar and Cyrus, (Daniel 4:34; Ezra 1:1-4), as a prelude to His future objective.

Even in the time of Ester God exercised His sovereignty as He impacted upon the mind of the king (Ester 6:1) and many Persians, at the time, converted to Judaism (Ester 8:1) through a reverential attitude towards the people of God.

The greatest hint with respect to the Father's plan for the imminent inclusion of the Gentiles into the grand scheme of Divine reconciliation was the coming of the Magi to worship the Messiah.

Originating from a great distance towards the East of Israel, the souls of these men were so impacted that they were given the knowledge of the imminent birth of the Savior of all mankind.

After paying homage to the Son of God, these men of the East were redirected to their homes, by Divine providence. This was done to ensure that the truth of the Gospel could be broadcasted in their distant world. (Matthew 2: 1-12).

> "For God so loved the world that he gave his only begotten
> Son, that whosoever believeth in him should not perish, but
> have everlasting life."
>
> John 3:16

Through the advent of Jesus Christ to the Earth, the master plan is made available to all men, Jews and Gentiles alike.

Any man could be included into the family of God, through the perfect blood that was shed on a hill in Calvary.

In this regard, the indigenous Indians of North America would not be omitted from receiving God's love. The Amerindians of South America and the Caribbean region would also have the opportunity afforded by everlasting life.

The Africans and East Indians would be edified by the Gospel of God's kingdom and would not perish through idol worship. Even the people of the Orient would be exposed to the WAY, TRUTH, and the

LIFE, so too the residents of the inaccessible mountains of Nepal and Tibet.

The universal plan of Almighty God which was elucidated even before the Earth came into being, is all-inclusive, encompassing every race and every tongue and would gather ALL things into one.

For those peoples who were so isolated that they were never exposed to written scripture, and for those people who have never heard of Jesus Christ, Almighty God made provisions by inserting, from birth, the Breath of Life. This serves as an inner witness of the existence of a Supreme Being. As the indigenous person submits to the yearning of this inner witness, an intimacy with Divinity is accommodated that the Calvary experience makes available to every human being.

Now that we have arrived at this juncture, has the eternal plan of God suddenly come to a halt? Many theologians would have us believe that this is the case but why would Almighty God take us through so many stages of mankind's development and then have this present Age in suspended animation?

For the past two thousand years the Church has resigned itself to waiting for the reappearance of Jesus.

However a detailed look at the plan would reveal a progressive development where a specific stage enhances and elevates the previous one.

From Abraham, the Patriarchs, the Nation of Israel, the Prophets, Jesus Christ and the Apostles, one stage took up the mantle from the preceding one and developed the plan to a higher level.

It follows then, that any stage following the Apostles must accomplish greater works. Unfortunately, this has not occurred over the last two millennia. The entire concept of sonship has been missed by the Church, as we have settled for a watered-down version called Christianity.

"A little one shall become a thousand, and a small one a strong nation: I the Lord will hasten it in his time."

Isaiah 60:22

But this is the Age of sonship, (his time) the final stage in God's master plan. All that God had in His mind for man (Genesis 1:26), would manifest in these last days. (The Lord will hasten)

All that man has been taken through, for all of his history, would be completed and perfected so that the SON would finally emerge as the head of all creation. (ONE SON: A STRONG NATION)

This era is most important as it sets the stage for the second coming of our Lord, Jesus Christ. Except for the work of the Messiah, the coming Age, which is upon us, is most critical in the spiritual history of mankind.

The will of God must be done. With the success of each past era, God will ensure the fulfillment of these end times by the sons of God:

> "God, who at sundry times and in divers manners spake in time past unto the fathers by the prophets. Hath in these last days spoken unto us by his Son, whom he hath appointed heir of all things, by whom also he made the worlds."
>
> Hebrews 1:1-2

This is the final Age before the return of the King of kings. This is why this coming era would be so special.

Made up of young, vibrant warriors, these sons of God, who have not been tainted by any strains of religion, would take prayer, worship and praise to never-before-seen levels.

Their prayer lives would not be saddled with the saddening cries of victimhood, but with a boldness and confidence, they would release spiritual power that would shake the foundation of the spiritual realms.

Having a solid relationship with the King, these end time believers would deal directly with Almighty God, not unlike Adam. As with Moses, they will speak to the Ancient of Days, face to face.

No longer would there be prayer that is full of repetitions and blanketed in doubt, designed to impress onlookers with sweet-sounding words and phrases.

Signs and wonders would occupy the actions of these sons of the Most High. As they pray, the dead would arise, sickness and disease would disappear, immediately. Blind eyes will be opened, crippled limbs would be straightened.

No fear would hinder the prayer lives of these believers; they would possess a faith that would cause *mountains* to move from their places.

Their prayer would be far removed from the conventional utterances of today, and as they move by faith, their petitions would be answered without saying a word. They would understand that the intimacy they would live by would give them an in Jesus name power. They would not have to confirm their positions as sons of God by repeatedly uttering in Jesus Name, but by their very appearance, demons would take flight.

The worship to come would operate on a level that would see entire communities fall under the power of the Holy Ghost. The worship of the Age of sonship would escape the formalities of church worship. The end time worshippers would cause changes in the atmosphere, spiritually. The worshipers will be selfless, consciously dead to their surroundings and completely taken over by the Holy Spirit.

No human words would be able to express the level of spirit involved in the worship, but a heavenly music communication would be attained that the human mind would not be able to contain or process. New songs would emerge that will not come from music sheets filled with chords and notes, but will be spontaneously created, as the worshippers yield everything to the Spirit.

As the sons of God lift their hands in reverence to their Father, all of creation would join in achieving unison of spirit that will go beyond present levels of understanding.

This is not an attempt to portray an air of spookiness or mysticism but the Spirit is hinting that in time to come, the praise and worship would be so different to what applies today, that it will challenge and stretch our imaginations.

Our God is a great God; all things are possible to Him. Almighty God's level of understanding is way beyond the way we process our thinking. What we do know is that the present ways of serving God would be discarded as the new season of enlightenment would render our activities inoperable and useless.

A purity of spirit would characterize the Age and the sons of God will exhibit a brilliance that would rival the sun.

This brilliance would be a crucial counter to the level of evil and satanic activity that would also escalate to previously unforeseen depths.

As man begins to flow in his true identity, the sonship of man will kindle a process that would oversee the return of perfection to all life.

What Adam missed out on, the sons of God would relish taking the task to even greater heights, than in the Garden of Eden. With the destruction of all the nature of evil, the spirit of sonship would continue to be for all times.

From the onset of creation, through the sonship nature of man, the physical territory was originally designed to develop in the spirit of sonship. This ensured the righteous progress through which creation would evolve and the same spiritual nature would characterize the earth, as it was in heaven.

But as Adam misunderstood his responsibility, as the prototype of a son of God, the earth has been progressively metamorphosing under a different spirit. Creation has not been in synchronization with the Spirit of heaven and in this regard, life on earth has been degenerating to supreme levels of disorder and ungodliness.

Through these circumstances, the present *gathering* cannot function at a true capacity and is incapable of directing creation to its righteous existence. Under the present religious spirit by which the 'church' operates, it has reneged in its responsibilities of leading the world towards the Fatherhood of God.

This is a perfect history-long scenario set by God so that the SON can arise out of the ashes of fiendish disorder and unrighteous chaos. As the SON strives in the role given by the FATHER, the world would once again flourish in the spirit of sonship.

> "But when the fulness of the time was come, God sent forth his Son, made of a woman, made under the law, To redeem them that were under the law, that we might receive the adoption of sons, And because ye are sons, God hath sent forth the Spirit of his Son into our hearts, crying, Abba, Father."
>
> Galatians 4:5-6

Reference List

All scripture is taken from the King James Version of the Holy Bible (copyright 2002 by Thomas Nelson, Inc.).

1. Lexicon Universal Encyclopedia #3, pg. 542, Conze, Edward "Buddhism: Its Essence and Development.
2. Lexicon Universal Encyclopedia #7, pg.32, Dix, Gregory, "The Shape of the Liturgy", 2nd ed (1945).
3. Lexicon Universal Encyclopedia #12, pg.376, Grell, Karl G, "Protozoology" 2nd rev, ed (1973).
4. Lexicon Universal Encyclopedia #9, pg.12, Bok, Bart J, and Priscilla F, "The Milky Way" 4th ed. (1974).
5. Lexicon Universal Encyclopedia #12, pg. 336, K. Aa Strand.
6. Lexicon Universal Encyclopedia #7, pg. 141, Black, JB, "The Reign of Elizabeth" 2nd ed. (1959).
7. Lexicon Universal Encyclopedia #10, Pg. 126, Hoskins, WG, "The Age of Plunder: King Henry's England 1500-1547" (1976).

About the Author

Alfred Prescott was born on the island state of Trinidad and Tobago, the most southerly isle of the archipelago of islands that make up the Caribbean. He is the only boy child of parents: Alfred Rogers and Velma Prescott, having two sisters: Donna Lyder and Marilyn Williams.

For the first ten years in the lives of the young Prescott siblings their religious upbringing was traditionally fashioned after the Anglican Catholic trend of the late 1960's and early 1970's on many of the islands of the British-influenced West Indies. His mother, as so many mothers of the era, insisted that her children become active members of the nearby All Saints EC church. Alfred distinctly remembered the pride etched on his mother's face when she learnt that both he and Donna were accepted as members in the then famous All Saints choir.

The religious atmosphere of the Prescott household, however, was changed forever when, in 1972 or 1973 Alfred's mother was introduced to Nicheren Daishoshin's Buddhism. With unbridled passion, Velma embraced her new found faith and made sure all of her children, particularly her only son, Alfred, were indoctrinated into the many chants and rituals of this Eastern religion.

Even at a young age, Alfred never liked the practice. With his protest of the annoying sounds of the constant ringing of the gong and the smoked filled rooms caused by the burning of incense, a point of contention was created between mother and son. Even though, Alfred studied all of the literature of the Buddhist belief, he never embraced the religion as had his siblings, who continue the practice to this day.

In 1986, Alfred met Sharon Jordan and in the following year they became husband and wife. This proved to be significant because it not only resulted in three beautiful children: Tricia, Darren and Stephen but 1998 Alfred accepted the Lord, Jesus Christ, into his life, as his wife had done seven years previously. They both became members of a full gospel, spirit-filled, talking-in-tongues, Pentecostal-type church.

In 2007, Alfred and his family moved on to fulfill the will of their heavenly Father with the "Sons of God Fellowship", a non-religious, non-denominational church which is dedicated to unifying the global body of Christ through Spirit- led, kingdom-of-God spiritual activities.

Alfred continues to grow in his purpose in the kingdom of God and has been anointed to write two books on spiritual matters. The first book "The Fatherhood of Almighty God" was published in 2012 and this present literary contribution, "In the Spirit of Sonship", will be the second in a long line of books that may bring edification to the global body of Christ.

Printed in the United States
By Bookmasters